TRACING YOUR ANCESTORS THROUGH DEATH RECORDS

FAMILY HISTORY FROM PEN & SWORD

Birth, Marriage and Death Records
David Annal and Audrey Collins

Tracing Your Channel Islands Ancestors
Marie-Louise Backhurst

Tracing Your Yorkshire Ancestors
Rachel Bellerby

Tracing Your Royal Marine Ancestors
Richard Brooks and Matthew Little

Tracing Your Pauper Ancestors
Robert Burlison

Tracing Your Huguenot Ancestors
Kathy Chater

Tracing Your Labour Movement Ancestors
Mark Crail

Tracing Your Army Ancestors
Simon Fowler

A Guide to Military History on the Internet
Simon Fowler

Tracing Your Northern Ancestors
Keith Gregson

Your Irish Ancestors
Ian Maxwell

Tracing Your Scottish Ancestors
Ian Maxwell

Tracing Your London Ancestors
Jonathan Oates

Tracing Your Tank Ancestors
Janice Tait and David Fletcher

Tracing Your Air Force Ancestors
Phil Tomaselli

Tracing Your Secret Service Ancestors
Phil Tomaselli

Tracing Your Criminal Ancestors
Stephen Wade

Tracing Your Police Ancestors
Stephen Wade

Tracing Your Jewish Ancestors
Rosemary Wenzerul

Fishing and Fishermen
Martin Wilcox

Tracing Your Canal Ancestors
Sue Wilkes

Tracing Your Lancashire Ancestors
Sue Wilkes

TRACING YOUR ANCESTORS THROUGH DEATH RECORDS

A Guide for Family Historians

Celia Heritage

Pen & Sword

FAMILY HISTORY

First published in Great Britain in 2013 by
PEN & SWORD FAMILY HISTORY
an imprint of
Pen & Sword Books Ltd
47 Church Street
Barnsley
South Yorkshire
S70 2AS

ISBN 978 1 84884 784 2

A CIP catalogue record for this book is
available from the British Library.

Typeset in Palatino and Optima

Printed and bound in England by
CPI Group (UK) Ltd, Croydon, CR0 4YY

Pen & Sword Books Ltd incorporates the Imprints of Pen & Sword Aviation, Pen
& Sword Family History, Pen & Sword Maritime, Pen & Sword Military, Pen &
Sword Discovery, Wharncliffe Local History, Wharncliffe True Crime,
Wharncliffe Transport, Pen & Sword Select, Pen & Sword Military Classics, Leo
Cooper, The Praetorian Press, Remember When, Seaforth Publishing and
Frontline Publishing

For a complete list of Pen & Sword titles please contact
PEN & SWORD BOOKS LIMITED
47 Church Street, Barnsley, South Yorkshire, S70 2AS, England
E-mail: enquiries@pen-and-sword.co.uk
Website: www.pen-and-sword.co.uk

CONTENTS

This book is dedicated to my Mother
who first kindled my interest in family history so
many years ago.
Mary Heritage
1927–1993

ACKNOWLEDGEMENTS

Although my name alone appears on the cover, many people have helped in the writing of this book. My warmest thanks are extended to the following, who kindly spent much time reading through various chapters and offering advice: Stewart Gillies of British Library Newspapers, Nicholas Rheinberg of the Coroners' Society, Dr Andrew Gray of the Heraldry Society, Audrey Collins of the National Archives, Michael Gandy, Chris Paton, Jayne Shrimpton, and Dr David Wright. Also a special thank you to Dr Carolyn Huston, with whom I exchanged many late-night emails and who opened my eyes to the likely interpretations behind so many causes of death!

My family, friends and fellow genealogists on Twitter and elsewhere have offered not only moral support and encouragement, but have also helped track down useful examples and images; though sadly there was not room to include them all. Particular thanks to Ann Ballard, Pat Brady, Jackie Depelle, Christine Goulding, Brenda Green, Jan Feist, Ann McDermott, Barbara Meredith, Helen Parkhurst of the World Burial Index, Lynn Sharpe, Pam Smith, Shirley Smith and to my client HC Zachry, whose family tree has provided some excellent examples for the book.

Images permissions were also gratefully received from Ivychurch PCC, Preston and Kendal Record Offices, Ancestry, LMA, Findmypast, TheGenealogist and Scotlandspeople. Thanks to staff at LMA, IHGS, SOG, Worcester Record Office, to Beth Snow of The Genealogist and Amy Sell of Findmypast for their help during my research and also to www.markrobinsonphotography.co.uk for photographic advice and enhancements.

One of the most time-consuming parts of writing a book is proofreading and here I owe a big debt of gratitude to Jayne Holtom for her help. I would also like to thank Emma Jolly for giving me the push to approach Pen and Sword with my idea for the book and to commissioning editor Rupert Harding for his patience in answering my regular queries!

Whilst I acknowledge the help of all of the above the responsibility for any errors or omissions, of course, remains solely my own.

My final and biggest thank you has to go to my husband Jonathan Risby, without whose help and support I could not have written this book.

INTRODUCTION

Family history has been part of my life since I was fifteen, and like many people I was initially preoccupied with trying to trace my pedigree as far back as I could. Once I had found one set of ancestors I had to find the next: it very quickly became addictive. As I progressed with my research I started to realize that there was a lot more to family history than just collecting names and dates and drawing up a family tree. I started to become interested in the places they had lived, and in discovering exactly what they did for a living. With this came a growing awareness that it was also useful to buy death certificates. One of my ancestors had died of typhus; another was killed by lightning, while the cause of death on my great-great-grandmother's certificate was 'Bad leg 14 years! General decay from age.' Fascinating stuff!

But it was not until ten years ago, when I stumbled across the premature death of my ancestor Edwin Barnes, that realization dawned. Records connected to an ancestor's death, such as death certificates, inquest records, obituaries, wills and gravestones are vital. They often shed more light on a person's life than those records actually created during their lifetime. In my ignorance I had totally overlooked Edwin's death and its consequences. He had in fact died as a result of a tragic accident at work and his death had had a devastating effect on the family. Tragic as this was, my discovery yielded a wonderful amount of information about the family; far more than any other documents ever had. Most importantly, it helped me to see the family in a new and much more realistic light. It seems an irony that it is often records of *death* that bring our ancestors to life more than any other!

It's all very well tracing your ancestors from their birth or baptism, through to their marriages and the production of their own offspring, but so many of us leave it at that and fail to follow our ancestor's lives through to their end. How can you really know your ancestor if you have no idea of how he died or what life was like for him in his later years? Family fortunes fluctuated and circumstances changed as the years went by. If you desert your ancestor at the time when he appears on his last census return or baptizing his last child, you are probably missing out on a vital chunk of your family history. If you are serious about your family history then 'killing off' your ancestors is mandatory.

In this book I aim to lead you through the various types of death records available and not only show you how to access them, but also how to get the most from them. In many cases you can use them as springboards for furthering your family research in other areas.

Finally, in the chapter entitled 'Repercussions of Death', I take a look at death itself and the knock-on effects it could have for the rest of the family; not just the immediate family, but potentially the family to come for the next few generations.

Although this book primarily concentrates on research into English and Welsh ancestors, where applicable I have tried to highlight any significant differences in the equivalent Scottish and Irish records at the end of each chapter.

Before we start, please note that to save making the text unduly cumbersome, I have used the pronouns 'he' or 'him' in the generic sense to denote our ancestors in general rather than repeatedly writing 'his or her' or 'he or she'.

Tips for Research

County Record Offices

When carrying out your research you must think of the UK in terms of its historic county boundaries. County boundaries have not remained constant and many places have found themselves in different counties at different times. Substantial changes in the names and boundaries of some counties occurred in 1974, but for family history purposes you will usually find counties listed by pre-1974 names and boundaries. You can find details of these at www.genuki.org.uk/big/Britain.html. Some parts of what we consider to be London were in Surrey, Kent or Essex until 1889 when they became part of the County of London and there were further changes in 1965.

Many of the records you will use in your research among death records are to be found at county record offices. These are usually located in the county town of each county, although many counties have more than one record office. The Archon directory at www.nationalarchives.gov.uk/archon/default.htm will help you locate the contact details for each office, but sometimes it is simpler to use an internet search engine and search on the name of the county you are interested in plus the term 'record office'. Before you visit, it is important to check that the records you are looking for are held at that particular record office. There are sometimes anomalies whereby records you think will be there are housed elsewhere. Although most record offices have their own online catalogues, many are not complete and not particularly user-friendly. It is worthwhile using them in tandem with the Access to Archives (A2A) catalogue at www.nationalarchives.gov.uk/a2a. This provides archival listings from 418 record offices around the country and sometimes contains information not available in the online catalogues of individual record offices. If you do not find what you are looking for on either of these it is worth checking with record office staff, who may have access to more complete listings.

Research at the National Archives in Kew

Making your first visit to the National Archives at Kew (TNA) can be a slightly daunting experience, but don't let this put you off. Before you visit make sure you have read the 'Visit Us' section on TNA's website. This will tell you how to prepare for your trip and what you need to take with you.

Document reference numbers at TNA are usually made up of three parts. The first part is formed of a letter or letters: the 'department code'. These refer to the department that originally created the document, for example, ASSI (Assize Court), C (Court of Chancery), BT (Board of Trade). The second part is the 'series number' or 'series code' and identifies a particular series of documents within that department. This usually consists of one set of numbers and is added to the department code, for example, BT 159: these are the 'Registers of Deaths at Sea of British Nationals'. The third part of the reference is called the 'piece number' and defines a particular document or set of documents within the series, such as BT 159/1, which relates to the 'Registers of Deaths at Sea of British Nationals in England between 1875 and May 1877.'

Keep up to Date with what is Available Online

Genealogy websites are constantly evolving as new datasets are released. One of the best ways to keep up to date with what is new is to subscribe to the newsletter of genealogy sites such as Findmypast, Ancestry and TheGenealogist. Most also have Facebook pages and Twitter accounts where they will post details of new data releases. Alternatively, subscribe to a newsletter that does a regular round up of internet releases such as my own Heritage Family History newsletter (email celia@heritagefamily history.co.uk) or that of Chris Paton at www.britishgenes.blogspot.co.uk.

It is very important to make sure you are familiar with any internet databases you search. Be clear as to which years and which records they cover: read the small print! Many titles give the impression that the database is all encompassing when it is not.

Using Records in Tandem with Each Other

One of the hardest aspects of researching death records is actually locating them – for reasons that are discussed in the book. Bear in mind that there is a considerable cross-over in the basic information provided by many of them, in terms of indicating when and where someone died or was buried. So, if you find it hard to locate one record you may well be able to track it down by using another type of record. There are, for example, many online databases covering memorial inscriptions. Searching those may lead you to a missing burial entry or vice versa, while a burial entry may provide a date of death and lead you to a death certificate, or an obituary in a newspaper may lead you to all three! Similarly I have located many deaths using the online index of the Principal Probate Registry, described in Chapter 6, rather than starting with a search in the General Register Office (GRO) death index. The probate index provides far greater detail of the deceased, making it easier to identify the correct entry with certainty when compared with the sparse details given in the GRO index. The downside of course is that many people did not leave a will and may not be mentioned at all. This highlights how important it is to use sources in tandem, not only to get as full a picture as possible of your ancestor and his life, but also to maximize the number of records you find relating to his death. As we shall see these often lead on to other records.

Family Records

Make sure you have searched your own family archives, whether this be the contents of your own attic or cupboards or those of a relative: you just never know what records may have been kept relating to the deaths of family members over the years. If you are lucky you may discover many of the records described here with little effort.

Family Search and the IGI

The Family Search website contains some of the most useful databases for family history research in general, both in the UK and overseas. The website is run by the Church of Latter Day Saints (LDS) and all their databases are free to use. LDS headquarters is in Salt Lake City, Utah, but they also have a massive record office in London and smaller Family Search Centres dotted throughout the world where you can order microfilm copies of parish registers and view databases such as the GRO index. A list of local Family Search Centres can be found at https://familysearch. org/locations. It also has a massive collection of online data relating to births, baptisms, marriages, deaths and burials from around the world at www.familysearch.org. Most importantly for UK researchers this includes what used to be known as the 'International Genealogical Index' (IGI). The IGI is a large collection of parish register transcriptions. Although it contains very few burial entries, it can be very important for tracing family members who have moved away from the home parish. The index is not complete by any means, however. Coverage can be ascertained on a parish by parish basis using the *Phillimore's Atlas and Index of Parish Registers* (Phillimore, 2003). The Family Search database has recently been upgraded and the IGI now forms part of its 'England, Births and Christenings, 1538–1975' and 'England, Marriages 1538–1973' databases. Apart from this, Family Search also has a growing collection of other UK records; both digitized images and transcriptions.

Locating Resources: GENUKI and Cyndi's List

Few people who begin to research their family history realize the amazing range of sources and subject matter that their new hobby covers. Likewise, few researchers ever fathom the depths of all the records available; it helps to know where to look when you require further information, however. For this GENUKI (www.genuki.co.uk) is one of the most useful websites for UK research, providing a virtual reference library of links to genealogical information relating to various sources, subjects and geographical areas within the UK. Similarly 'Cyndi's list' is an American-based site but with links to genealogical sources and topics from around the world (www.cyndislist.com). Both websites are free.

QUICK REFERENCE: ABBREVIATIONS AND WEBSITES

The nature of this book means there are frequent references to various websites, archives and organizations. In order to avoid repetition these are listed below, as are any frequently used abbreviations.

Abbreviations

A2A	Access to Archives
DDR	Death Duty Register/s
FFHS	Federation of Family History Societies
GENUKI	Genealogy UK and Ireland (see Tips for Research)
GRO	General Register Office
GROIRE	General Register Office of Ireland
GRONI	General Register Office of Northern Ireland
IGI	International Genealogical Index (see Tips for Research)
LDS	Church of Latter Day Saints
NAI	National Archives of Ireland
PRONI	Public Record Office of Northern Ireland
NAS	National Archives of Scotland
NRS	National Records of Scotland
TNA	The National Archives, Kew

Commercial data providers

Ancestry	www.ancestry.co.uk
BMD Registers (also available on TheGenealogist)	www.bmdregisters.co.uk
Familyrelatives	www.familyrelatives.com
Findmypast	www.findmypast.co.uk
Findmypast Ireland	www.findmypast.ie
TheGenealogist	www.thegenealogist.co.uk
Origins Network	www.origins.net
ScotlandsPeople	www.scotlandspeoplehub.gov.uk

Other Genealogy Websites

FreeBMD   www.freebmd.org.uk
GENUKI (Genealogy UK and Ireland)   www.genuki.org.uk
   This very useful free site provides a virtual reference library of genealogical information relating to the UK and Ireland.
Family Search   www.familysearch.org

Archives and Libraries

Access to Archives (A2A)   www.nationalarchives.gov.uk/a2a
ARCHON (Directory of Record Offices)
                         www.nationalarchives.gov.uk/archon
British Library   www.bl.uk
General Register Office (GRO)   www.gro.gov.uk
General Register Office for Northern
  Ireland (GRONI)   www.nidirect.gov.uk/gro
London Metropolitan Archives (LMA) www.cityoflondon.gov.uk/lma
The National Archives (TNA)   www.nationalarchives.gov.uk
National Library of Wales   www.llgc.org.uk
National Library of Ireland (NAI)   www.nationalarchives.ie
Public Record Office of Northern
  Ireland (PRONI)   www.proni.gov.uk
General Register Office for Scotland www.gro-scotland.gov.uk
National Archives of Scotland (NAS) www.nas.gov.uk

   The last two organizations merged in April 2011 to form the National Records of Scotland (NRS). At the time of writing their websites still operate independently and there is also a temporary website for NRS as below. A new NRS website is currently under development and should be up and running by late summer 2012. The former National Archives of Scotland and General Register Office for Scotland websites will be closed down when all relevant information and content is accessible via the new website
National Records of Scotland   www.nrscotland.gov.uk

Organizations and Institutes

Federation of Family History Societies (FFHS)   www.ffhs.org.uk
Institute of Heraldic and Genealogical
  Studies (IHGS)   www.ihgs.ac.uk
The Scottish Association of Family
History Societies (SAFHS)   www.safhs.org.uk
The Society of Genealogists, (SOG)   www.sog.org.uk

Chapter 1

DEATH CERTIFICATES

For many of us, either starting out on our quest to trace our family history, or even as more experienced researchers, death certificates may not seem a priority. We have a natural desire to extend our family tree backwards: once we find one generation we feel compelled to discover the next. While birth and marriage certificates directly help us do this, death certificates do not. They are also expensive and therefore we often regard them as a luxury, rather than an essential part of our research. They are, in fact, a very important part of our studies and should not be overlooked. Whether an ancestor died a dramatic death, or passed away quietly in his bed, a death certificate can add an enormous amount to what we know about him and his family; in fact it can be one of the most rewarding of death records for the family historian.

We often terminate the research into our ancestors at the point they appear on their last census return or at the birth of their last child, perhaps believing we have found all there is to know about them. But their circumstances could change dramatically in the intervening years before their death, and a death certificate often reveals much about the circumstances of their lives in later years. Knowing how your ancestor met his end is part of learning all about him and you will also often learn more about his family too, especially in terms of how his death affected them. Sometimes, although the deceased may have been greatly mourned, his death will have had few direct consequences. In other cases it may have had a devastating effect on the family.

Another good reason for locating your ancestor's death is that, once you find it, you will not waste time searching for him in records after this date. From 1969 death certificates are also helpful in locating the birth of your ancestor, because they contain details of his place and date of birth. They are also particularly useful for ancestors born after 1911, for whom no census is available from which to determine the person's age or place of birth. Finally, they may also provide crucial details about an ancestor's rank and regiment if he was in the army, which can be vital for further research in other records.

Death certificates were introduced to England and Wales on 1 July 1837 as part of the new system of civil (state) registration of births, marriages and deaths administered by the General Register Office. Similar systems were introduced to Ireland on 1 January 1864 and Scotland on 1 January 1855 and we shall look at these later in this chapter. From these respective dates onwards you should be able to locate a death certificate for each of your ancestors using the death index for each country. The death certificate is, however, often the hardest to locate of the three certificates that plot the course of our ancestors' lives. The reasons for this will be explained later.

The introduction of the civil registration system of births, marriages and deaths to England and Wales in 1837, and the corresponding systems that followed on from this in Scotland and Ireland, were revolutionary in two ways. Firstly, apart from a brief attempt to introduce a locally organized civil registration system of births, marriages and deaths during the rule of Oliver Cromwell, it was the first time that the state, rather than the church, had undertaken the recording of the nation's vital events. Previously it had been the church that was responsible for recording the key milestones in a person's life, in the form of baptisms, marriages and burials. Secondly, the information collected was treated as a national rather than a local record, and indexed accordingly. This makes it far easier to trace a family that moved from one area to another.

What Death Certificates Tell You

An English, Welsh or Irish death certificate is divided into numbered columns and provides the following information:

1. Date and place of death
2. Name of deceased
3. Sex
4. Age at death
5. Occupation
6. Cause of death
7. Who registered the death and their address
8. When the death was registered
9. Signature of the registrar

It is very easy to concentrate solely on the cause and date of death and to give little thought to the rest of the information on the certificate. However, with a little care you can get a lot more from it. Let's take a detailed look at the English death certificate, using the death certificate of my ancestor Ann Barnes as an example.

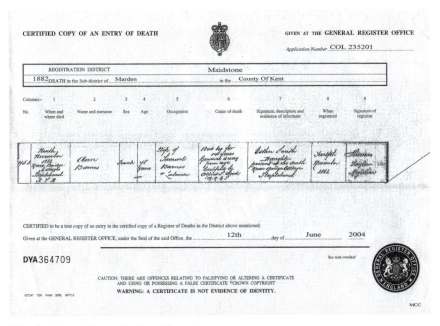

The death certificate for Ann Barnes.

Column 1: Date and Place of Death

The place where your ancestor died can give an insight into both the circumstances of his death and his family life. Although it may simply give the name of the village where your ancestor died, in many cases an actual address will be recorded. The address on Ann's certificate is 'Knox Bridge Cottages, Staplehurst R.S.D.' 'R.S.D.' stands for 'Rural Sanitary District', which was a type of administrative unit created in 1875 in England and Wales and in Ireland three years later. In 1894 (1898 in Ireland) they were replaced by Rural and Urban Districts, and you will see the abbreviations 'RD' and 'UD'.

If a full address is given, consider if it is familiar to you from other documents. Your family may have stayed in the same location for years or could have moved frequently, so a little investigation may be needed to determine whether your ancestor died at home or elsewhere. Ensure that you have compared it to the address given on your ancestor's last census return and to any other documents relating to him and to the wider family. The address on Ann's certificate was very familiar to me from census records and told me that she died at home, in the house she had lived in for the majority of her married life.

If the death was registered by the deceased's spouse then check to see if

3

the address given for him or her in column seven is the same as that in column one. If it is, then your ancestor almost certainly died at home. Once one half of an elderly couple had died the remaining parent often moved in with one of the children, so the other common scenario is that the address at which they died was that of a son or daughter. However, if this particular child did not register the death this may not be immediately apparent. Alternatively, your ancestor may have lived with a more distant relative or a friend in their final years.

To find out more about an unfamiliar address, locate it in the decennial censuses either side of the year of death to see who was living there. If the death is more than a year or so before or after a census year the inhabitants may well have changed, but your search may reveal another branch of the family living there with whom your ancestor went to live in old age. This is where it pays to study your *complete* family tree rather than to concentrate solely on your direct line!

Addresses on Death Certificates: Taking it Further

Although the address on a death certificate may read like a normal street address it could be an institution such as a workhouse or nursing home. By the beginning of the twentieth century there was a growing tendency not to refer to workhouses directly as such. Woolwich Workhouse in Kent, for example, was often recorded on certificates as '79b Tewson Road, Woolwich'. In 1913 workhouses were renamed 'Poor Law Institutions' and in 1930 they became 'Public Assistance Institutions'. Many were given euphemistic names to disguise their origins and these may appear on the death certificate, either with or without a street address. Southwell Workhouse in Nottinghamshire was known as 'Greet House' from 1913, while my great-grandmother Emily Heritage died in 1924 in the 'Central Home', Leytonstone, which had been the workhouse up to the end of the First World War.

Peter Higginbotham's website www.workhouses.org.uk provides extensive information on the location and background to workhouses throughout the United Kingdom, as well as listing which records survive. Sometimes it is the death certificate that provides the first reference to your ancestor's stay in the workhouse and this can lead to further information from workhouse records. You may find he was regularly admitted over the years or perhaps removed from one poor law union back to the union where he had 'settlement' ('settlement' referred to the place that was responsible for a person if he required poor relief). The death certificate for William Smee, a chair mender from Deal in Kent, showed he died in 1885 in the local workhouse at Eastry. I initially assumed he went into the workhouse when his health failed in later life, but research into the workhouse admission and discharge records showed that he had been regularly in and out of the workhouse for a number of years.

If your ancestor died in a hospital the 'Hospital Records Database', which can be found on the website of the National Archives (TNA), provides information on almost 3,000 hospitals past and present in the United Kingdom. The list is not comprehensive, but includes the whereabouts and dates of records for each hospital listed, although patient records are normally closed to public inspection for 100 years. The site is searchable both by place name and hospital name and if you simply search using the word 'workhouse' this will bring up a list of all hospitals in the database that were previously workhouses.

You can also use old maps, trade and post office directories to find out more about an address, including who lived there and its exact location. A larger scale Ordnance Survey (OS) map (six inch or twenty-five inch) will indicate if there was a workhouse in the street where your ancestor died that may account for his address at death. The local library or archives for the area will hold copies of old OS maps and TNA has a good collection on the shelf in its map room. Many old maps are available as reasonably priced reprints from companies such as www.alangodfreymaps.co.uk, www.oldtowns.co.uk, and www.cassinimaps.co.uk.

By the start of civil registration in 1837 there were directories for most towns and for some rural areas too. From the 1850s geographical coverage is good and they became increasingly popular up to the Second World War. Trade directories were usually known by the name of the publisher, such as *Kelly's*, *Pigot's*, *Bulmer's* etc, while by the late nineteenth century the Post Office published its own directories listing the majority of residents in an area. Directories vary in format depending on their date, and the publisher; they also vary in the geographical area covered in each volume. Some may cover just one town, but others a far wider area. By the late nineteenth century many directories contained separate sections listing tradesmen according to their trade, then residents by name and finally residents by address: the last will be a real boon for your research.

The good thing about later nineteenth-century and early twentieth-century directories is that, unlike the census returns, they were often published annually and make a more accurate source for determining who was living at an address in a particular year. Bear in mind that, because there was a delay between gathering and collating the information for each directory and its actual printing, directories could be six months or a year out of date by the time they were published. It is therefore worth looking at a directory for the year before your ancestor died rather than the year of death itself.

KELLY'S
CHANNEL ISLANDS PRIVATE RESIDENTS
DIRECTORY.

(The initial letter G. is to be used for Guernsey & J. for Jersey).

Abbott Thomas, Seaton place, Brock road, St. Peter Port
Acourt John, St. Ouen, J
Adair Rev. Philip, 22 Vauxhall st. St. Helier
Adams George, 3 St.Luke's cottages, Elizabeth street, St. Luke's, J
Adams Mark, 2 Endsleigh place, Gibauderie, St. Peter Port
Adderson Mrs. South Lynne, St. Saviour's road, St. Helier
Agnew Alfred M. St. Thomas place, Grange road, St. Peter Port
Agnew Charles Edward, 69 Hauteville, St. Peter Port
Agnew Gerald William, Wintonia, Guielles road, St. Peter Port
Agnew Mrs. 4 Victoria crescent, St. Peter Port
Agnew Thomas Hilary, 69 Hauteville, St. Peter Port
Ahier Chas. 34 Green st. St. Helier
Ahier Charles, St. Clement, J
Ahier Charles P. St. Clement, J
Ahier Frederick, Eton lodge, Don road, St. Helier
Ahier J. 10 Winchester st. St. Helier
Ahier Miss,14Havre Des Pas,St.Helr
Ahier Mrs. 4 Clarence terrace, Clarence road, St. Helier
Ahier Mrs. 5 Springfield crescent, Trinity road, St. Helier
Ahier Mrs. Philip, Wivel ho. George Town road, St. Luke's, J
Ahier P. La Ferme, St. Martin, J
Ahier Peter, 4 Dongola rd. St.Helier
Ahier Philip,19 Chevalier rd.St.Helr
Ahier Thomas, 3 Hillside, Wellington road, St. Helier
Aikman John M.D. Birnam, Queen's road, St. Peter Port
Alavoiné Adrien, St. Saviour, J
Alavoine M, 7 Parade rd. St. Helier
Alavoine Max, Stirling castle, Les Vaux, St. Helier
Alexander George, 3 St. Mark's crescent, St. Mark's road, St. Helier
Alexander Misses, Plymton villa, Rohais road, St. Peter Port
Alexandre Giffard P. 32 La Motte street, St. Helier
Alexandre John, St. Brelade, J
Alexandre Josue, St. Aubin, J
Alexandre Matthew John, Hawkmount, St. Brelade, J
Alexandré Miss, Grouville, J
Alexandre Miss, 3 Trafalgar terrace, New St. John's road, St. Helier
Alexandre Mrs. Franc Fief, St. Brelade, J
Alexandre Mrs. 37 Roseville street, St. Helier
AlexandrePhilippe-Brocq,St.Ouen,J
Alexandre.W.C.TheOaks,St.Peter, J
Alfred W. R. La Cheaumer, Castel,G

Allaire Miss Dora Le B. La Grands Courtils, St. Saviour's, G
Allardice Mrs. 1 Norfolk terrace, Rouge Bouillon, St. Helier
Allen James D. C. Hirzel house, Smith street, St. Peter Port
Allen Mrs. 34 Parade pl. St. Helier
Allés Miss E. Bon Air, St.Martin, G
Allés Mrs. Mary Rachel, Casrouge, Forest, G
Allez John, Gazel, St. Martin, G
Allez Misses, Canichers, St.Peter Port
Allez Mrs. Les Buttes, St. Saviour,G
Allez Mrs. Mary, 95 Mount Durand, St. Peter Port
Allis Mrs. La Pre, St. Peter-in-the-Wood, G
Allix F. 7 Havre Des Pas, St. Helier
Allix Richard, 12 Commercial bldgs. St. Helier
Allix R. 17 Havre Des Pas,St.Helier
Amedroz Capt. L. E. 54 Hauteville, St. Peter Port
Amies The Misses, 39 Mount row, St. Peter Port
Amy Adolphus, Navarino ho. Stopford road, St. Helier
Amy Adolphus, 13 St. Clement's rd. St. Helier
Amy Alfred, Villiers place, Bagot road. St. Luke's, J
Amy George, Gorey, J
Amy Henry, 1 Ravenswood villas, Green street, St. Helier
Amy Jean,Buckingham ho.Grouvll.J
Amy Jean, St. Aubin, J
Amy J. Les Arches, St. Saviour, J
Amy Mrs. 1 Croydon villas, Cleveland road, St. Helier
Amy Mrs. 15 The Terrace, Grosvenor street, St. Helier
Amy Mrs. Elizabeth, Gorey, J
Amy Mrs. J. 4 Livingstone villas, Stanley road, St. Peter Port
Amy Mrs. Marie, St. Martin, J
Amy Philip, 3 Halkett villas, Belvedere, St. Luke's, J
Amy Philippe, St. Martin, J
Amy Philip-Du-Parcq, Grouville, J
Amy Thomas P. Clermont, Rouge Bouillon, St. Helier
Anderson Charles John, Feckenham, Queen's road, St. Peter Port
Anderson Edouard, St. Saviour, J
Andrews Charles Thomas,1 Belgrave terrace, Dicq road, St. Helier
Angel H. R. Cordier vil.St.Peter Pt
Angell Tom,1 Woodbine villas,Bagot road, St. Luke's, J
Anglis Robert, Fontenay lodge, George Town road, St. Luke's, J
Angus James S. Elretiro, St. Saviour's road, St. Helier
Anthoiné Thomas, St. Saviour, J

Annesley Miss, St. Thomas place, Grange road, St. Peter Port
Arnold E. C.,M.A.Cantab.Elizabeth college, Grange road, St. Peter Pt
Arnold Frederick Henry, 1 Stanley villas, Stanley road, St. Peter Pt
Arnold William John, Amballes rd. St. Peter Port
Arthur Adolphus John, St. Ouen, J
Arthur J. Five Oaks, St. Saviour, J
Arthur James, 3 Ocean view, Almorah road, St. Helier
Arthur Jean, St. Mary, J
Arthur John Le Couteur, St.Mary, J
Arthur John S. St. Mary, J
Arthur Mrs. Clara, St. Mary, J
Arthur Mrs. Mary, 2 L'Hyvreuse villa, George Town rd. St.Luke's,J
Arthur Miss Sophie, St. Mary, J
Arthur Robert, Grouville, J
Ashplant —, La Maisonette, Cobo Bay, Castel, G
Asplet P. Berlin villa, St. Peter, J
Aubert Mrs. Vine grove, Mount Durand, St. Peter Port
Aubert Philip, Millbrook, J
Aubert P. J. 31 Val Plaisnt.St. Helr
Aubin Alfred Jackson, Belle Vue, Lower King's Cliff, St. Helier
Aubin Clement Lerrier, 1 Windsor crescent, Val Plaisant, St. Helier
Aubin John T. 5 Don rd. St. Helier
Aubin John Wm. St. Clement, J
Aubin Mrs. 21 Duhamel pl.St.Helier
Aubin Mrs. 28 Roseville st. St. Helr
Aubin Mrs. St. Peter, J
Aubin Percy, Caledonia house, New St. John's road, St. Helier
Aubin Philip A. Sunnyside, Claremont hill, St. Helier
Aubin Philippe, Parkfield, Trinity, J
Aubin Thomas M.D. 39 La Motte street, St. Helier
Aubin W. Duret, 15 & 17 Duhamel place, St. Helier
Auburn Mrs. 54 Don road, St. Helier
Auger Mrs. Lamorana, 36 Mount Durand, St. Peter Port
Auvergne Mrs. Bon Air,Green lanes, St. Peter Port
Averty Fras.P.36 Don rd. St. Helier
Baal Abraham, St. Martin, J
Baal Abraham, jun. St. Saviour, J
Baal Richard,Sergente, St. Martin,J
Backhouse Mrs. 2 Springfield crescent, Trinity road, St. Helier
Badier John Billot, St. Martin, J
Bagnell Miss, Casa Melita, Doyle road, St. Peter Port
Bailhache Philip,Mont Cantel,Rouge Bouillon, St. Helier
Bainbridge Miss, 10 Clarendon road, St. Helier
Baker Edward, Chaumiere, Sark

1889 Directory of the Channel Isles. By the late nineteenth century many directories included separate sections listing tradesmen by trade and residents by name and address. (Image reproduced by courtesy of TheGenealogist www.thegenealogist.co.uk)

Directories will be found in local libraries and archives for the area in question, while many are now available online as part of the subscriptions offered by commercial genealogy companies and for purchase as CDs. The University of Leicester has many English and Welsh directories available for free viewing at www.historicaldirectories.org/hd/index.asp.

Electoral rolls began in 1832. They list all voters by address and may help to identify who your elderly ancestor was living with. The British Library has a large collection of electoral rolls for the United Kingdom and a very helpful online research guide. Others will be found in local libraries and archives, while some are online at Ancestry (London), Family Search, Findmypast (Cheshire) and British Origins (Somerset). Not everyone was included on the electoral roll, however, and there are partial gaps in the listings during the First and Second World Wars. *Electoral Registers 1832–1948 and Burgess Rolls* by Jeremy Gibson (The Family History Partnership, 2008) is an essential guide for locating the correct registers.

Columns 2 and 3: Name and Sex

Most surnames have variant spellings and your ancestor's name may be spelled differently from the way in which you have seen it in other documents or from what *you* regard as the correct spelling of your family's name. We will look at this in greater detail in the section on what to do if you fail to find a death entry. Very occasionally you may find that someone has been given the wrong sex. This is usually simply a clerical error!

Column 4: Age

The age at death can be helpful and problematic at the same time. Together with other records, such as census returns and ages on marriage entries, it can be used as a basis for locating the correct birth or baptism. This is especially helpful if you are researching a more popular surname and are faced with a choice of birth entries, or if you are researching someone who was born before the introduction of birth certificates in 1837 and died before the 1851 census, which was the first to record ages more accurately. It can, however, also lead to confusion. Ages on death certificates are notoriously inaccurate, especially if the person died in old age. This often occurred when a death was registered by a grandchild, or son-in-law or daughter-in-law who was less familiar with facts about the deceased. If your ancestor's death was registered by someone who was not a relative, such as the workhouse master or an employee, then this is even more likely. In some cases you may find that someone close to the deceased got it wrong. Ann's death is registered by her daughter, but is still one year out; Ann was actually seventy-seven when she died, not seventy-eight. An obsession with birthdays and dates of birth is a relatively modern phenomenon, so even Ann may not have been aware of her true age. If your ancestor was illiterate he would not have been able to read the date on his birth certificate and would rely on what he had been told, or what he thought he had been told. Where possible, compare your ancestor's age on *all* documents you have found to see if it remains consistent. If it fluctuates repeatedly then he was probably unsure of his age and you need to widen your search in birth or baptism records accordingly. Where an ancestor's age on the census returns has changed from year to year, the death certificate may help clarify the situation. Despite the slight inaccuracy, the age on Ann's certificate was still helpful in tracking down her baptism, and in Ann's case the baptismal entry also gave her date of birth.

Column 5: Occupation

You will normally have an idea of the job or profession that your ancestor followed from other records such as census returns or a marriage certificate. The occupation given on an ancestor's death certificate may help confirm that you have identified the correct death. On the other hand you may find a sudden and unexpected career change has taken place, and this may cause you to wonder whether you have found the right person! Don't make the mistake of presuming that because your ancestor has appeared in earlier records as an agricultural labourer, for example, he cannot be the same person who died with his occupation noted as carter or wine cellarman. These are all unskilled jobs and need no special training. Someone on a lower income doing unskilled work would have taken any better paid work as and when it became available. It is important to bear in mind that there was mass migration from the countryside into the towns during the Industrial Revolution as jobs on the land dwindled and jobs in towns doubled. Even after the advent of state pensions for the over-seventies in 1908, and contributory pensions in 1911, many of our ancestors had to work well into old age in order to provide for themselves and their spouse. In many cases your elderly ancestor would have downgraded or changed his job for something less strenuous. My great-grandfather ran a nursery and florist's business for many years, but on his death certificate he is shown as a 'jobbing gardener'.

Many middle-class ancestors could afford to branch out and take on new business opportunities. For example, your ancestor may have started off as a butcher or baker, but later taken on the tenancy of the local inn as well. Many people simultaneously ran more than one type of business and they would not necessarily all be listed on the death certificate. One of my ancestors combined the trades of draper, grocer and innkeeper, while my

| Nineteenth December 1934 3 Weir Bank. Kendal HD | Agnes Dickinson | | Female | 66 years | Spinster, a Drapers Shop Assistant (Retired) Daughter of John Stewardson Dickinson a Corn Miller (deceased) |

The death certificate for Agnes Dickinson provides her father's details despite the fact that she was sixty-six when she died.

husband's ancestor, Charles Curling, was variously a 'tailor', 'coffee shop keeper' and 'comedian'. On his death certificate his widow described him as an 'actor'. The reliability of information given on a certificate was dependent on the accuracy of the person who supplied it. There are many examples of the informant inflating the description of the deceased's occupation or status, while the way we describe occupations today may differ from terms used in previous centuries.

If the certificate was for a child, the father's details will be shown in this column. For a woman this section is less about her than about the man in her life! She will usually be described in terms of her relationship to her husband (wife or widow of so and so) or, if she was unmarried, to her father – even if she died in old age. The occupation of the husband or

Agnes and Barbara Dickinson. (Author's collection).

9

father will usually also be given. Although I already knew that Ann was the 'wife of Samuel Barnes a labourer', this told me he was still alive in November 1882 and helped me narrow down the period of time in which I had to search for Samuel's death.

It was not until the twentieth century that women's occupations were routinely entered on death certificates, and this depended to a large extent on the information given by the informant. Two of my great-great-aunts, Agnes and Barbara Dickinson, died as spinsters between 1934 and 1939. Each had her own career and the corresponding death certificates give details of their occupations as well as their spinster status. What is surprising, however, is that the certificates also record details of their father's name, despite the fact that he had been dead since 1881 and the ladies were aged sixty-six and sixty-seven respectively when they died.

Column 6: Cause of Death

This is one of the most interesting parts of the certificate. Many people rule out buying death certificates because they will only 'tell me that my great-grandfather died of old age'; yet relatively few certificates list 'old age' as the sole cause of death. Ann's certificate states that she died of 'Bad leg for fourteen years. General decay from age'. The terminology here is vague, but the detail about her leg is food for thought. Initially it may be hard to understand how a bad leg could have killed her, but we can try to read between the lines. She may well have suffered from osteoarthritis, or varicose veins; the latter would have been quite normal following a hard life as a labourer's wife during which she spent much time standing. By contrast, she could have had an injury to her leg. As she grew older her leg may have become ulcerated and this, together with her increasing age, may have helped hasten her decline. Whatever the actual cause, this told me that she must have endured pain and inconvenience in the last fourteen years of her life; a life that was probably hard enough already. It pays to take time to consider the information on the certificate thoroughly, and specifically in relationship to that particular person. How would any illness or condition have affected his or her life? What impact would this have had on the rest of the family?

You may find that the terminology used for the cause of death means little to you, while in many cases it can be open to misinterpretation by modern readers. A helpful leaflet entitled *Causes of Death and Old Medical Terms* is available from www.genealogyprinters.com, while useful websites include www.scotlandsfamily.com/medical-diseases.htm and www.antiquusmorbus.com. The latter is a very good site with lots of details, although being American may contain some differences to British medical terms in early records.

The way in which causes of death were recorded changed over the years.

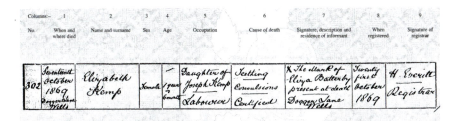

The cause of death given on the certificate for baby Elizabeth Kemp records the symptoms of her illness rather than the cause of death.

Up to 1845 causes of death on certificates were rarely certified by a doctor and this led to some very vague descriptions provided by the informant, who usually had no medical knowledge and described the symptoms as he perceived them. If a doctor had been called in to see the deceased before he died, then the informant might have had an idea of what was wrong with the person, but doctors were expensive and many families would not have been able to afford one.

In 1845 the General Register Office (GRO) sent out standardized medical forms to doctors for the purpose of certifying deaths, but many remained uncertified because a doctor was simply not in attendance. From this date onwards the certificate should state whether the cause of death was certified or not. Doctors were encouraged to use a list of diseases compiled by the GRO as part of its drive towards the use of specific terminology that related to the actual *cause* of a person's death, rather than merely describing the apparent symptoms, or attributing it to external factors such as, for example, 'cold'. Despite this many certificates still recorded the symptoms of the illness rather than the cause of death, such as that for baby Elizabeth Kemp, who died in 1869 of 'Teething' and 'Convulsions'.

From 1875 all deaths had to be certified by a doctor, although you may occasionally see an uncertified certificate in the years immediately after this, where the registrar failed to follow the correct procedure. The cause of death should also be followed by the doctor's name and qualifications. The registrar was not allowed to issue a certificate until he had received a medical certificate from the doctor stating the cause of death. From 1875 a doctor was only able to complete this if he had been in attendance on the deceased during his final illness *and* had seen him either within the last fourteen days of his life or immediately after death. In 1893 this was clarified further. The doctor had to have seen the deceased at least twice within the fortnight prior to the death and one of those visits had to have been within the last eight days. If there was no doctor qualified to sign then the death had to be notified to the coroner.

Although some of the terminology used regarding the cause of death may appear scientific, in some cases it does not actually indicate the cause of death; only the doctor's lack of knowledge! 'Syncope', which is technically defined as 'a sudden loss of consciousness', was often used to describe sudden deaths, especially on early certificates; but it leaves the reader no wiser as to the cause, and is a reminder that nineteenth-century medicine was far less advanced than that of today. Doctors were unable to give an accurate diagnosis for many diseases. 'Miasma' was similarly meaningless, and referred to the belief that noxious vapours in the air caused certain types of illnesses, ranging from bronchitis through to malaria. 'Dropsy' is also found as a cause of death, although it actually describes the symptoms of death. These would have included large levels of fluid retention, which would have left the patient extremely uncomfortable due to the swelling of the internal organs and often the legs. If the lungs were affected they would also have had problems breathing. The actual cause, however, would usually have been heart failure, kidney or liver disease. Another term that was sometimes used to explain the gaps in a doctor's knowledge was 'Visitation of God' and, although this would seem to indicate a sudden death, such as that caused by a heart attack or possibly a stroke, this may not always be the case.

Some terms sound confusingly similar but mean very different things. 'Typhoid fever' is easily confused with 'typhus' and, although both are infectious fevers, the former is characterized by septicaemia, a rash and intestinal irritation, and the latter is characterized by headaches and delirium. While typhus is spread by the bites of ticks and fleas, typhoid fever is spread by contaminated water or food.

Tuberculosis

If you see 'phthisis' or 'phthisis pulmonalae' as the cause of death on a certificate then your ancestor died of tuberculosis. Phthisis derives from a Greek word meaning 'decay' and referred to the wasting effect that the disease had on the body, as did the other frequently found term 'consumption'. The term 'tabes mesenterica' indicates tuberculosis of the abdomen and is usually caused by drinking unpasteurized milk from cattle with bovine TB. Other symptoms usually included a bloody cough, general lethargy and a fever. TB is not hereditary but is caused by a bacterium that produces small growths that initially start in the lungs. However, it has many different forms and could spread elsewhere in the body. In its pulmonary form it was easily spread through the air and other members of a household were at great risk of infection. The disease could lie dormant in the body for many years and in some people never developed into full-blown TB. Two of my great-uncles, Charles and Thomas Heritage, both died of the disease as young men in 1909. Even though they had long left

---

home by the time they died, it is possible that they had both developed the disease while still living with their parents.

The disease was rife in the UK into the twentieth century and, although the number of people suffering or dying from the disease declined as sanitation and living conditions improved, a satisfactory treatment was not found until the 1950s.

From the early 1900s you may see causes of death listed numerically on certificates. This was introduced to provide a more logical recording of the various diseases that caused death, which could be more easily used for statistical purposes.

1a was the actual cause of death
1b indicated any underlying cause of the final illness
1c indicated the cause of the final illness
2   indicated any other illness that contributed to, but did not cause the death

These would be used as appropriate by the doctor, who was also supposed to indicate the length of any illness on his medical certificate. This was not always added to the death certificate, however, while the accuracy of the doctor's certificate (even in the twentieth century) still depended on how meticulous the doctor was.

Although the majority of our ancestors will have died as a result of illness or disease, you may be surprised just how many of our forebears died a violent or unexpectedly sudden death. The forty-third Annual Report of the Registrar General shows that in 1866 15,094 deaths were classed as 'accidental' or 'negligent' and a further 1,329 as 'suicide'[1]. I look at this in greater detail in Chapter 4. Historic causes of death may still affect your family today and I look further at this in the chapter on 'Repercussions of Death'.

Column 7: Signature, Description and Residence of Informant

This can often be one of the most informative columns in terms of helping us find other family members. The 1836 Registration Act required that 'some Person present at the Death or in attendance during the last Illness' should register the death or, if no one fitted this category, then it should be registered by the occupier of the house or the inmate (if the occupier had died).[1] This was amended in the 1874 Registration Act to read 'it shall be the duty of the nearest relatives of the deceased present at the death, or in attendance during the last illness . . .' to register the death, with a similar rejoinder that, in their absence, the duty should fall to the occupier. From this time onwards any relationship between the informant and the deceased should be stated. The informant on Ann's certificate is her daughter Esther Smith who was 'present at the death'. This was an important piece of information. Esther proved to be a missing twelfth child who had not appeared on any of the census returns with her parents, and whose birth I had therefore failed to locate. The certificate showed that she lived in the same row of cottages as her parents and provided her married name. It took only a few moments to locate her, her husband and children on the census and to add a new branch to my family tree. 'Present at the death' shows that Esther was with Ann when she died, although I am sure this phrase would also be used if the informant was in the house, but not actually in the same room as the person when they died.

You will also see the phrase 'in attendance'. This indicates someone who had been caring for the deceased in their final days, but who was not present when they actually died. From 1875, you will occasionally see the informant described as the person 'causing the body to be buried'; this indicates someone who was organizing the funeral where there was no family member to do so.

Case Study: The Elusive Christiana Beck

If a married daughter registered a death it is often an easy short cut to discovering her married name and potentially a new branch of the family in the census returns.

My great-great-aunt Christiana Beck was born in 1874. I was unable to locate a marriage or a death for her. The death certificate of her father John, who died in 1915, showed the informant to be 'C. Mitson daughter'. Since he had no other daughters with names beginning with this initial, this had to be her! By searching for a marriage between a 'Mitson' and a 'Beck' I was able to identify her marriage under the forename 'Christina', which she seems to have used from adulthood instead of Christiana. I also located an earlier marriage for her and three children, thus successfully bringing down all lines from my great-great-grandparents down to the twentieth century.

Although you may have little interest in tracing other branches of your family, it can help put the lives of your direct ancestors into context and show you how they interacted with other family members. You may find important scraps of information about your own ancestor in documents relating to other relatives. For example, a new address might be recorded when they registered the death of a relative.

If the person who registered the death was not a family member, it could be a friend, servant, neighbour or the head of an institution such as the workhouse. Again, using the nearest census return to locate the person may help you work out how they were connected. Sometimes you may find that the informant was actually related, even though this is not stated. The registrar would have entered the relationship as given to him by the informant, who may have not considered his relationship to be close enough to warrant a mention. In most cases the informant will have lived nearby, and it should not be too difficult to identify him in census records. You may conclude that he was simply a friend or neighbour, but even this will help you build up a picture of your ancestor's later years.

The other person who may be shown as the informant is the coroner and this is one of the classic cases where the humble death certificate can lead to a wealth of other material concerning your family. Deaths were notified to the coroner in certain circumstances: if the death was sudden, unexpected or suspicious in any way then he would have to be informed. The coroner would consider the circumstances of the death and decide whether or not to call an inquest. In some cases the coroner would decide that an inquest was not required. (See Chapter 4 for further details.)

Column 8: When Registered

Although the date of registration is usually of little importance, it will show if there was any delay registering the death and, if there was an inquest, give you an idea of how long it lasted. This will help provide a time frame in which you can search for newspaper reports.

From 1969 the date and place of birth is also given on the death certificate and the maiden name of a married woman or widow.

Ann's death was not dramatic in any way and the certificate does not provide some of the marvellous springboards for further research that often accompany the certificates of those ancestors who have died accidental or sudden deaths. It did, however, provide me with a lot of extra information about her: it confirmed her approximate year of birth, which helped me to find her baptism, it helped narrow down the date of death of her husband and led me to a branch of the family tree I would probably never have discovered otherwise. It also gave me an insight into what life had been like for Ann before she died and showed that she had died at home, in the place where she had lived for the majority of her life.

Locating and Buying Certificates in England and Wales

There are two separate indexes to birth, marriage and death registered in England and Wales. The first is the index made at local level by each district register office and the second is that made by the General Register Office (GRO), which collated entries on a national level. The latter is compiled

Case Study: Who Registered The Death Of Mary Dickinson?

My widowed ancestor Mary Dickinson died in 1857 in Kendal, Westmorland, aged seventy-three. Her place of death was given as 'Beast Banks', which is the name of a street. The name and address of the informant was 'E. Dobson', who also lived in Beast Banks. I wondered if this could be Mary's daughter Elizabeth, who was born in 1807, or simply a neighbour.

Since this was a pre-1875 certificate no relationship would have been recorded. I checked the 1851 census which showed that 'E Dobson' was indeed called Elizabeth and she was also born in 1807. The census showed that she was a schoolmistress and wife of William Dobson, a twine spinner. There was, however, one piece of evidence that seemed to indicate she might not be my Elizabeth. Whereas baptismal evidence indicated that my Elizabeth was born in the village of Selside, Elizabeth Dobson gave her place of birth as Crosthwaite, some fifteen miles away. Although it was feasible that Elizabeth could have been born in Crosthwaite but baptized in Selside, I needed to find evidence to prove her identity beyond doubt. I checked other census returns which confirmed her place of birth, while the 1841 census showed that William and Elizabeth had a young son called Joseph. I decided to buy his birth certificate as this would give Elizabeth's maiden name. The certificate showed that Elizabeth Dobson's maiden name was 'Fleming' not 'Dickinson', and therefore it was just a coincidence that she was the same age as Mary's daughter Elizabeth. Mary's cause of death was given on the certificate as 'apoplexy 24 hours', which probably indicates a stroke. I can now be fairly certain that Elizabeth Dobson was simply a friendly neighbour who probably kept an eye on elderly Mrs Dickinson and who was there for her in the last hours of her life.

from copies of the original district register office entries that were sent on a quarterly basis to the GRO. It is useful to have an understanding of how the GRO index was compiled, as this will help you understand why, on occasion, you may fail to find an entry you are looking for.

When the system of civil registration was introduced to England and Wales in 1837, the country was divided for this purpose into twenty-seven regions, and each was given a number. Kent, for example, was given the number 'five' while Cumberland, Westmorland and Northumberland were allocated the number 'twenty-five'. This regional number is important because it played a part in the indexing process, and forms part of the reference number you use when you order a certificate from the GRO. The regions were based on administrative units created in 1834 for the new poor law system, and were divided into 619 registration districts, many of which were further divided into sub-districts. Each registration district was headed by a superintendent registrar, while a sub-district was headed by a registrar of births and deaths. The region numbers and registration districts were altered in 1852, 1946 and 1965. A useful set of maps showing the various regions, registration districts and their relevant numbers is available from the Institute of Heraldic and Genealogical Studies (IHGS).

From 1 July 1837 every death had to be registered with the registrar of the sub-district where the death occurred. Entries were recorded in books and, when these were full, they were passed to the superintendent registrar for the district. Deaths were supposed to be registered 'as soon as possible'; within eight days was the norm up to 1875 when new legislation stipulated 'five days'. This might be extended where there was an inquest or post-mortem.

Four times a year each registrar had to make copies of all deaths in his sub-district and send them to the superintendent registrar, who was supposed to check them for accuracy. He then sent these quarterly returns to the GRO office in London, and it was the information in these copies that was used to form the national index.

Once at the GRO office the quarterly returns were bound into numbered volumes. The volume number related to the relevant region number from which that set of records originated. So all records received from superintendent registrars in Kent were bound into a volume numbered 'five' and those from Northumberland, Cumberland and Westmorland into a volume numbered 'twenty-five'. Then the index was compiled.

The GRO index is ordered by year and divided into three sections according to the type of event: birth, marriage or death. From 1 July 1837 to the end of 1983 each year is also divided into quarters. The four quarters of the year are correctly referred to by the last month of each quarter:

March:	Deaths registered between 1 January and 31 March
June:	Deaths registered between 1 April and 30 June
September:	Deaths registered between 1 July and 30 September
December:	Deaths registered between 1 October and 31 December

Remember that the criterion used to allocate a death to its correct quarter is when the death was registered, not when it occurred. Therefore, if the death took place towards the end of a quarter, it might be registered in the following quarter. Similarly it might be registered in the first quarter of the following year if the death occurred towards the end of December. You may see the quarters referred to numerically as Q1 (March), Q2 (June) etc.

In order to create the death index (and similarly the birth and marriage indexes) every vital event from all of the register offices in England and

17

Wales had to be sorted into alphabetical order each quarter. This was done by copying each entry out again, onto pre-printed pages containing the appropriate registration district name and volume number. The pages were then cut into slips and sorted manually: it was these that were used to create the final index. When complete, the index for each quarter was bound into three large books (one for each type of event), and each entry included not only the person's name and the registration district, but also an allocated reference number. This reference number was formed of the volume number, which related to the bound volume where the entries for that region were kept, and also a page number, which indicated the page of that volume in which the entry would be found. It is these details that tell the clerk who issues your certificate where to look for an entry.

Creating the index was a massive task and mistakes inevitably occurred, not only when the index was created, but also at local level when the original copies were made by the registrars. The records held at district register offices are more accurate than those held by the GRO because they have not been repeatedly copied.

SURNAME of Deceased Person	NAME of Deceased Person	SUP. REGISTRAR'S DISTRICT	Vol.	Page
Dickens	William	Wellington	3	697
Dickens	William Thomas	Stamford	7a	185
Dickenson	Elizabeth	Manchester	8	d141
Dickenson	Jane	Malton	9	d264
Dickenson	John Castle	Huddersfield	9	a188
Dickenson	Mary	Gloucester	6	a164
Dickenson	Mary Sheet	Wirral	8	a278
Dickenson	Matilda	Birmingham	6	d120
Dickenson	Samuel Walter	W Bromwich	6	b379
Dickenson	Sarah	Mile End	1	c406
Dickenson	William	Grantham	7a	275
Dickenson	William Fredric	Barton	8	c518
Dicker	Ann	Newton Abbott	5	b93
Dicker	Eliza	Basingstoke	2c	111
Dicker	Elizabeth	Wokingham	2c	236
Dickerson	Ann	Royston	3	a128
Dickerson	Elizabeth	Foxhoe	4	b159
Dickerson	Ellen	Walsingham	4	b251
Dickerson	Esther	Stroud	6a	212
Dickerson	John	Cambridge	3	b321
Dickerson	John George	Kensington	1	d161

An extract from the December quarter of the GRO Death Index for 1857. (Image reproduced with the kind permission of findmypast.co.uk)

Ages were only included in the index from 1866. Identifying deaths before this date can be difficult, especially if the surname is popular or extremely localized. A date of birth is given in the index from 1 April 1969, thus helping identify the correct entry – provided the informant gave the correct information!

Up to 1866 all a person's forenames were included in the index, if they were supplied by the informant. After this date policy has changed several times as to how many forenames should be recorded in full, rather than merely as initials. In 1866 and between 1 July 1910 and 31 March 1969 the first name was written out in full, but any other forenames were reduced to initials. Between 1867 and 30 June 1910 and from 1 April 1969 the first two forenames were given in full plus any other initials.

The majority of websites that offer the GRO index allow you to search for a death by inputting your ancestor's name into a search engine. This makes it relatively easy to search over a wide period of time for the death where necessary.

If you know exactly where, and have a good idea of when a death took place, it is sensible to apply to the relevant district register office for a copy of the certificate as their entries are less prone to copying errors. You should not, however, expect register office staff to search for your ancestor's death if you have little idea of when he died. Some offices do provide a facility whereby you can pay for a search in the records, but many are unable to offer this service. It is advisable to check the website of the register office in question to see which services it offers. Also be aware that you cannot use a reference number you have found in the GRO index to order a certificate from a local register office. It will not be compatible with their index. If you know sufficient details to apply for a certificate, the easiest way to find out which register office covers the place where the death took place is to go to www.ukbmd.org.uk/genuki/reg or to look on the government's website at www.direct.gov.uk. Registration districts have changed over the years so check that it holds the records you seek. Many register offices are now part of a scheme (UKBMD) whereby register office indexes are being made available online for free, as a result of the work of volunteers. These indexes can be found at www.ukbmd.org.uk and it is well worth checking to see if the districts relevant to your research are covered. The indexes for some counties include the age of death in pre-1866 entries, whereas the national index does not.

For most of us, however, because we do not know exactly when or in which registration district our ancestor died, it is simpler to try and track down his death in the GRO index. This is currently available for events up to the end of 2006 on Findmypast (2005 on Ancestry, FamilyRelatives and TheGenealogist) or on microfiche up to the end of 2011 at the following places:

Birmingham Central Library
Bridgend Reference and Information Library
City of Westminster Archives Centre
Manchester City Library
Newcastle City Library
Plymouth Central Library
The British Library

The government information website at www.direct.gov.uk provides up to date information on where you can view the GRO index. It does not, however, list the various Family Search Centres (run by the Church of Latter Day Saints) to be found throughout the UK. These also hold fiche copies of the index and details of the centres can be found at www.family search.org/locations.

For the majority of people the most convenient way to access the index is via the internet. Websites that offer the index are listed under 'Commercial Websites' in the 'Quick Reference' section at the start of the book and on the above mentioned government website.

Before ordering a certificate it is advisable to check the details of the entry on an actual image of the original GRO index page rather than relying on a transcription, just in case the website has incorrectly transcribed an entry. Most websites offer this facility.

Although FreeBMD does not yet offer images of all index entries (click on the pair of spectacles where available to view an image), it is an excellent site and the quality of its transcription is generally good. The site is free and although its index is not yet compete (being work in progress) most years have been fully transcribed up to about 1950 (as of May 2012). There are a few odd gaps before this so it is advisable to check the coverage charts available via the home page before you search. Ancestry uses the same FreeBMD index on their website up to the end of 1915. The nice thing about using the FreeBMD site is that you can easily filter your results by county or by registration district, which is useful when you are looking for a common surname, or where you are sure that a death has taken place in a certain area. Read the help page (available from its main search page) for details of how to get the most from its search engine.

Once you have identified the death you are searching for, you will need to order the certificate. No further details will be available to you unless you do so. This currently costs £9.25 or £10 if purchased from a local register office. Many people wonder why researchers are forced to buy an actual copy of the certificate when all they want to do is to see the information. This is because of the wording of the 1836 Registration Act, which stated that information could only be given in the form of certified copies of entries.

Certificates can easily be ordered online via the government's official ordering website at www.gro.gov.uk/gro/content/certificates. Be wary of ordering certificates through other websites, which may charge an extra fee.

For deaths before 1984 you will need to note the name as entered in the index, the registration district name, page and volume number as well as the year and quarter to order your certificate. After 1984 you will need to enter the year and month of registration as given in the index. For deaths within the last fifty years you will also have to state the age at death. Either an age or date of birth (from which the age can be calculated) will be found in the index.

Ordering is straightforward, unless you cannot read the GRO reference number clearly. In that case try looking at an image of the index from another website or, if it is the volume number that is not clear, check one of the finding aids mentioned in the later section on locating missing deaths to identify the correct volume number for the district. Remember that this may vary according to the year.

You can apply for a certificate without quoting the GRO reference number if you know to within a year or two when the person died, and have a fairly good idea of *where* he died. GRO staff will search a three-year period, (one year either side of your quoted year) and use the details you supply to search for the correct entry. There is currently no extra charge for this and, if no entry matches, you will receive a full refund of the certificate fee. This can be useful where there is more than one potential death for your ancestor in the same registration district within a short space of time.

Identifying the Correct Death

Unless your ancestor has a particularly distinctive name, it is helpful to have an idea of when he died. Even someone with what you believe is an unusual name will have namesakes, so it pays to take care when identifying an ancestor's death in the index. For research up to 1911 your ancestor's death can usually be ascertained to within a ten-year period from the census returns. This census is the last currently available to the general public, however, and after this it becomes harder to locate death certificates unless you or a relative has personal knowledge of when a person died. The death of my ancestor Charles Chapman Heritage was easy to locate because of his distinctive middle name and also because he failed to appear on either the 1901 or 1911 census returns. A search of deaths between 1891 (the last census on which he appears) and 1901 soon revealed his death entry in the March quarter of 1901. My ancestor William Gage, born 1837, was more difficult, however. He appears on the 1911 census aged seventy-four, but since there is no census available to view after 1911 I could not be certain how much longer he had lived. Starting with the presumption that he had died before he was eighty, I found two possible deaths for a William Gage of the right age in the area in which he was living in 1911, namely Camberwell. The first certificate I ordered showed that this William had died in the workhouse and his death was registered by the workhouse master. I could not be sure that I had the correct certificate since it was not a relative that registered the death, and there was no familiar address with which to connect him. I therefore ordered the second certificate. When this arrived it was clearly the correct one. His death was registered by my grandfather, his son-in-law, and the address where he died was my grandparents' address.

Case Study: Locating the Correct Death Certificate for William Heritage

When searching for the death of William Heritage several years ago, I found three possible entries in the right period and place.

I knew William died between the censuses of 1841 and 1851 but, because no age is given in the death index at this time, I was unable to identify which death was likely to be his. If I had been able to travel to the record office to look for his burial I could easily have pinpointed the correct death certificate, but that involved a long journey. In the end it was cheaper to buy all three certificates! The first two certificates related to children, but the third appeared to be his. Although the age was out by five years, both his occupation and place of residence matched. William was unmarried and the informant appears to have been unrelated and may well have been unfamiliar with his true age. These days I could access Warwickshire burials online at Ancestry, which would have helped me identify the correct entry much more easily.

When using census returns to determine the period in which an ancestor died, don't stop at the first census for which he fails to appear, but check the next one as well, just in case he is alive, but unrecorded, in the previous one. You can also use other sources such as wills and trade directories to try and pinpoint his date of death more accurately. The National Probate Index, in particular, is sometimes a quick and easy way of locating a date of death after 1858 as it provides greater detail than the GRO index (see Chapter 6). Bear in mind that when someone disappears from a trade directory they might just have decided to stop paying for an entry in it, while they may still appear in it the year after they died, thanks to the delay between collating and publishing mentioned earlier.

No.	When and where died	Name and surname	Sex	Age	Occupation	Cause of Death	Signature, description and residence of informant	When registered	Signature of registrar	
234	Twenty second April 1917 Vale View Backbarrow Holker Upper R. D.	Jane Postlethwaite Wilson	Female	86 years	Widow of John Wilson Worker in Powder Factory	1. New growth of Stomach 2. Exhaustion Certified by E. T. Hawksworth L. R. C. S.	Harold Wilson Grandson Lowwood Haverthwaite Ulverston	Twenty second April 1917	William Cragg Deputy Registrar	In No. 234 Col. 2 for "Jane Postlethwaite . Wilson" read " Jane Wilson" and in Col 5. read "James Wilson" for "John Wilson". Corrected on 31st May 1917 by me William Cragg Deputy Registrar on the Authority of a Statutory Declaration made by Harold Wilson and Thomas Wilson.

The amendments made on the death certificate of my ancestor Jane Wilson show that both her name and the name of her husband were originally recorded incorrectly.

Incorrect Details

A death certificate is an official record and, as such, most researchers presume that the details on it will be correct. Sadly, this is not the case! We have already seen that the age at death and the perception of the cause of death may be inaccurate, because they were based on the data provided by the informant. Other inaccuracies may also occur. Registrars could also make mistakes when they completed the death entry: this might be anything from a mistake in the address, to the date of death, the person's name, occupation or the relationship of an informant.

Sometimes mistakes were corrected at a later date, but in many cases they were never picked up because the family was illiterate, or did not bother to have them corrected. An error could only be rectified following evidence, or a verbal declaration, from at least two credible witnesses. In that case the original entry would be annotated to show the correction. Take a look at the details on the certificate for my ancestor Jane Wilson, above. Not only is her name wrong ('Postlethwaite' was her maiden name, not her middle name), but the first name of her husband is also wrong, reading 'John' instead of 'James'. These mistakes were corrected after her grandsons provided a statutory declaration as to the true details. The details were also corrected in the GRO death index, although this did not always happen.

Building a Larger Picture through Death Certificates

It often pays dividends to investigate the lives of your ancestors' siblings. You will learn much more about your family in this way than if you merely study your direct line in isolation. Firstly, see if you can find marriages for your ancestor's siblings in the marriage index. If there are any that appear never to have married, or who disappear unexpectedly from the census returns, then look for their death. This can often provide an insight into some of the sadder events in your family's life. Some siblings died as infants or young adults, and your ancestor may not have grown up with the bevy of siblings for company that you had assumed. Two children of the same name is usually, but not always, an indication that an earlier child has died. Although many children died in infancy in Victorian times, and parents no doubt expected to lose some of their children, don't presume that they were totally resigned to this fact. Statistics from the year 1900 show that 100 out of every 1000 children born alive died before the age of one year.[2] There is no question that the loss of successive children, or the death of a child as a teenager or young adult, will have been a traumatic event for parents, and often for siblings too, even though in some cases it meant fewer mouths to feed and may have made life easier in this respect. Loss of the mother through childbirth was also still reasonably frequent at the start of the twentieth century. Some six to nine births out of every 1000 resulted in the mother's death. This will often be described as 'parturition' on the death certificate.

The death certificate for my great-great-uncle Tom Hemming, who died as a baby in 1846, showed that he only lived twelve hours. The cause of death was certified by a doctor and given as 'presumed malformation'. The informant was Tom's father Henry. The cause of death seems to indicate that the doctor suspected one of Tom's internal organs had not formed properly, but it could also indicate trauma to the brain caused during a difficult delivery. Tom's parents named their next child 'Frederic Tom', perhaps in his memory.

You may see certificates where a baby's cause of death is recorded as 'congenital syphilis'. If the mother had been infected with the disease, this was likely to be passed down to a child in the womb. The mother would initially suffer miscarriages and then stillbirths. The disease often became less aggressive with time, so after several years she would start giving birth to live children, but they might be blind or deaf, or suffer from a variety of other symptoms or deformities. Very often these symptoms did not show up until sometime after birth. After several more years she would eventually start producing 'normal' children again although, sadly, they might be infectious themselves. So if you have a family tree which seems to indicate this pattern, it is something that should be considered. Syphilis was very common until the introduction of antibiotics in the twentieth century.

The births of stillborn babies were not registered until 1927, and few questions were asked if a newly born baby was brought for burial which the parents declared to have been born dead. From 1875, however, a doctor's certificate was required before burial could take place. This was partly as a result of government concerns about infanticide of illegitimate babies.

Case Study: The Westwood Children – A Case of Death and Emigration

My great-great-aunt Margaret Dickinson married Joseph Westwood, a farmer, in 1881 in Ulverston, Lancashire and they had eleven children between 1883 and 1900. I tried to trace Margaret's descendants down to the present day, but I had surprisingly little success. I was only able to find the marriages of three of them, and this prompted me to start looking for the deaths of the others. Finding out more about what happened to them gave me a much deeper insight into the family's life.

Margaret and Joseph's first son, John, died as a young baby in 1886 and their third son, Stephen, of tubercular meningitis in 1901, aged twelve years. Margaret died three years later in 1904 and was spared the tragedy of the death of her fourth son, Joseph, in 1912. What a shock it must have been for Joseph senior, and his remaining children, when twenty-one-year-old Joseph was struck down and killed by lightning in the fields near their farm in Cark-in-Cartmel.

Of the eight remaining children two other sons emigrated to the USA. A blanket search of all records on Ancestry's worldwide database picked them up, firstly on passenger lists arriving in the USA, and later on the census returns. Once one family member went there was a far greater chance that other family members would follow.

Causes of Brick Walls

Many people fail to find the death certificate they are looking for: there are many reasons why this may be. Despite the fact that, from July 1837, a death certificate was required for a burial to take place, some clergymen were hostile to civil registration in its early years, and carried out burials without seeing the necessary certificate. This accounts for a small number of missing death registrations up to 1874, when the law was tightened up. Probably the most common cause of 'missing' deaths, however, is that the details are recorded, but not recorded as the researcher expects! We have already seen how ages could be recorded inaccurately, and it is important to allow for this when searching the index after 1866 when ages are listed.

Surnames and forenames may also be recorded in an unexpected manner. This may be a transcription error, either by the registrar (who may also simply have misheard or miscopied the name), the clerk who copied the information out to form the index, or by a modern transcriber when a new index is created for a website.

If you can't find an entry, search again using a different website. Most commercial websites offering the GRO index will let you search their indexes free of charge, so you do not need to subscribe or buy units to do this. If you find a likely entry, you can return to the website to which you subscribe and use the extra information you have learned (such as the year,

25

quarter and registration district) to locate it successfully, even if it has been badly transcribed.

Spelling was not standardized until as late as the twentieth century. Although you may have strong feelings that your family name is and 'always has been' spelled in a certain way, this is never the case. Everyone's surname has been recorded differently and probably in many variant forms over the years. This may range from the adding, removing or substituting of vowels or consonants, such as in 'Heritage', 'Heratage', 'Heretage', 'Hertage', 'Herritidge', or even the dropping or substituting of the first letter of the surname, such as 'Eritage'. Reflect on how many times people incorrectly hear or write your own name, sometimes recording a name they are familiar with rather than what they hear. Thus I have found myself referred to as 'Ms Hermitage' and even (this time due to someone's illegible handwriting) 'Ms Herbage'!

My great-grandmother's family name was 'Aley', but it can be found as 'Ayley', while another ancestor's surname is recorded variously as 'Hoppin', 'Oppin' and 'Orping'. If you have trouble locating someone with a name beginning with Mac or Mc check the variant spelling. Similarly, in names such as O'Connor the 'O' may have been omitted when recorded. While it is often not feasible to search under each possible variant, most search engines offer the facility to use a wildcard on any letter you suspect may have mutated. If you still have no joy, then it often pays to remove the surname completely from the search box and search on first name, approximate year of death and likely county or registration district of death. You may have to trawl through pages of results, but patience often pays off! If you have a good idea of when the death took place, another course of action is to browse the index by year and quarter rather than utilizing a search engine. In this way your eye may pick up the entry you are looking for on the same page, but spelled in a different way.

Forenames are also subject to change. Many people were known by their middle name and it may be this, rather than the name found on their birth certificate, or in census returns, that was recorded on their death certificate. If a grandchild registered a death he may have had no idea that granddad, whom he had always heard referred to as 'Bert', was really called 'Richard Albert', while 'Bert' could equally have stood for 'Bertram'. Similarly 'Nell' may have stood for 'Eleanor', 'Sally' for 'Sarah' and 'Peggy' for 'Margaret'. A useful book is *First Name Variants* by Alan Bardsley (FFHS, 2003). You may also find that a person's middle name has simply not been recorded. Names were also sometimes inadvertently reversed; so 'Henry James' might become 'James Henry', while a name might have been added at baptism that was never added to the person's birth certificate.

Variant spellings and mistranscriptions by modern website transcribers can often be overcome by patience and intuition. If a mistake has been made in the GRO index itself, however, this may be harder to surmount.

Mistakes in the GRO Index

Many researchers have a blind faith in the index. We have, however, already seen how it was compiled and how prone to error it could be. It pays to look at this in greater detail in order to illustrate some of the more common mistakes that may prevent you from correctly identifying the entry you require. Between 1998 and 2001 the New Zealand genealogist Mike Whitfield Foster carried out an in-depth study of the GRO marriage index, and the accompanying records held by the GRO, with staggering results. Although researchers long suspected inaccuracies in the index, it was his research that not only proved it, but showed just how inaccurate the index can be. Having said this, the marriage index is certainly more prone to error than the birth or death index. This is because the majority of registration was undertaken by the clergy, who were much less concerned with following the guidelines suggested by the government in terms of how data should be recorded than the registrars, and who were frequently negligent in sending in their quarterly returns! Despite this, many of the errors Mike found inevitably apply to the death index as well. The majority of these would be copying errors that invariably occur when large quantities of data are transcribed by hand. The problem for researchers is that it can be hard to spot when there is an error in the index. However, if you come to a point where you have carried out all other searches for the missing death possible, it makes sense to start working to the theory that the death has been incorrectly recorded or indexed.

Below is a list of the most likely causes of error in the index, with suggestions as to what can be done to overcome them.

- *Miscopying or mixing up of two lines of data*
  Thus a forename may be linked with the wrong surname. A search using the surname only may help overcome this, but will be reliant on the surname not being too common, and the researcher having at least a rough idea of when and where someone died.

- *Miscopying lines of data so that the name is linked to the wrong registration district name or volume number*
  You may still spot the entry but the issuing clerk may have problems locating it. If it is the registration district name that is wrong, it may well mean you fail to recognize the entry as the one you are looking for. Hopefully if the district name is wrong the volume number will be right and vice versa. This is a good reason to familiarize yourself with the registration district volume numbers applicable to the area your ancestors lived.

- *Transposing the first forename with the middle name*
  Fairly easy to overcome, especially when the surname is not a
  common one; for example ensure that you search for 'Henry
  James Burton' under 'Henry Burton' and 'James Burton'.

- *Incorrect sex!*
  You may encounter the occasional 'sex change' such as
  Theodora Dyer who appears in the index in 1846 as 'Theodor'!
  She is, however, recorded correctly on her certificate.

- *Misreading the surname*
  This might just involve the substitution of an 'e' rather than
  an 'a' or a 't' rather than a 'd' in the middle of the name,
  which would usually still render the name recognizable.
  However, if the original entry was in a particularly florid style
  of handwriting it was often the initial letter of the surname
  that proved difficult to interpret. Such an error might
  effectively create a totally different surname. A good example
  is the death entry for 'Susannah Pitcombe' who died aged
  ninety-five in the first quarter of 1919 in Wheatenhurst
  registration district. Her real name was actually 'Susanna
  Titcombe'. In this case her great age distinguished her entry,
  making it reasonably easy to locate. It is worth using a
  wildcard on the first letter of the surname, if the website you
  are using will let you do this, or substituting other first letters
  yourself if it will not. Misreading of first initials is less likely
  to happen to more common names that were easily
  recognizable to the clerk. Other examples of names changing
  beyond recognition include 'Butters' becoming 'Butler',
  'Waller' becoming 'Walter' and 'Sayer' becoming 'Sayel'.

- *Hyphenated surnames*
  These were generally indexed by the GRO under the first part
  of the hyphenation, so Smith-Jones would be indexed after the
  Smiths. This did not always happen, however, so it is wise to
  check under both parts of the name. In some cases the first
  part of the surname began life as a surname given as a middle
  name and was only later hyphenated by the family.

- *Double entries*
  This may not lead to a missing death, but it may confuse the
  issue. If there was doubt as to the way the name had been
  spelled in the original entry, the GRO clerks were supposed to
  enter the name in the index under both possible spellings. If

you find two entries, you can usually tell if they relate to the same person because the volume and page number will be the same. An exception to this might be where a father and son with the same name died in the same year, quarter and registration district and appear on the same page of the register. Before 1866 when no age was given in the index this would make them indistinguishable in the index.

The original GRO indexes were handwritten and remained so for many years. As the index became worn, it was gradually replaced by a type-written index. This meant that the index was copied out yet again and further copying errors introduced. Mike Foster showed that some pages of the marriage index were omitted when it was typed up, probably caused by the copyist turning over two pages at once. Further errors were caused by the fact that 'ditto' was normally used, instead of writing the surname out repeatedly for each entry. Occasionally the typist started on the fore-names for a new surname without remembering to insert the new surname. There is no doubt that all these types of errors occurred in the death index too.

In the Wrong Place!

Many people fail to find deaths because the entry they are looking for is not in the expected geographical location. Our ancestors moved around more than we give them credit for, and even a relatively short move could take them across a county border. Long-distance emigration could take your ancestor to the other end of the country, or even abroad. Either scenario can lead to a missing death.

It pays dividends to be aware of the location of registration districts and county boundaries. The set of civil registration maps produced by the IHGS clearly illustrates the location of the respective regions and registra-tion districts, and lists volume numbers. Studying these will help you decide how likely a death entry is, while a working knowledge of which volume numbers cover the expected area of death is useful, especially if you are not familiar with the names of the districts in the area. Two other useful guides are: *Registration Districts* by Ray Wiggins (3rd edn, SOG, 2001) and *A Handbook to the Civil Registration Districts of England and Wales* by Brett Langston (2nd edn, Family History Partnership, 2003). The former lists all registration districts, sub-districts and, very helpfully, all adjacent districts in England and Wales, while the latter lists all districts, volume numbers and dates of abolition where appropriate. Mr Langston has a similar listing on the GENUKI website via its civil registration pages, while www.direct.gov.uk also lists registration districts and volume numbers.

If you find an entry that matches in terms of its name, age and date, but is not where you expected it to be, it may be the case that your ancestor either relocated permanently before his death, or simply that he died while away from home. Those with jobs that involved travelling, such as commercial salesman, excise men, insurance salesmen or someone who worked on the railways come high on the list of candidates for this. Someone in poor health may have died in a hospital or sanatorium miles away from their home.

Many elderly parents went to live with their children, who might have moved some distance away from the area where they were born. Even your ancestor who died in the prime of life might have been living some distance from the family's original location, perhaps only temporarily. The case study of Edwin Barnes in Chapter 4 shows how, although born in Kent, Edwin and his family lived in London and then for a few years in Wales, before returning to London to live once more. If he had died while he was living in Wales, I am sure that I would have hesitated about buying the death certificate, because I had it in my head this was a 'south London family'. The family was there for such a short time that they do not feature on any Welsh census returns.

A death is usually registered in the district in which it occurs, but in exceptional circumstances, such as where there has been a major disaster, the Registrar General may give authority for the registration of the deaths to be shared between several neighbouring registration districts. So, once again, it pays to be up to speed with the location of registration districts. Your missing ancestor may have crossed over to Scotland or Ireland from England or vice versa, or to the Isle of Man. Similarly, many people from the south-west of England travelled to the Channel Islands to undertake seasonal work. So ensure you have checked the databases for all countries, where possible.

A significant number of our ancestors ventured overseas, often either to the colonies, or to America where opportunities seemed greater. Relaxation of restrictive British laws concerning shipping and the conveyancing of passengers in 1827 and 1828 led to cheaper fares, while the introduction of steam-powered ships in the 1850s greatly reduced sailing times, thus opening up overseas travel to all classes. Some people left the UK under local poor law schemes which offered assisted passage to the poor of the parish. These were at their height in the 1830s and 1840s, while assisted passage was also possible through the 'Colonial Commission of Land and Emigration', established in 1842. David Hey, writing in *The Oxford Guide to Family History* (Oxford University Press, 2002), states that the Commission had helped over 300,000 British citizens to emigrate by 1869. He estimates that some ten million British people emigrated in the nineteenth century and, while some returned, many died abroad. Although their deaths may have been registered in records belonging to the country where they died, not all such deaths were recorded in UK overseas records (see below). The problem faced by the researcher is his ignorance as to whether or not the ancestor in question actually left the UK and, if he did, where he went. If your family was poor, then inspection of local poor law records, notably any surviving accounts of the Overseers of the Poor and also vestry minutes, is always worthwhile and may shed light on an ancestor's departure. Some Colonial Commission records survive and are to be found at TNA.

Passenger lists for those people leaving the UK were kept by the Board of Trade from 1890 onwards and are available online at Findmypast up to 1960. These lists generally only cover long-haul sea journeys and not everyone will be listed. Some passport applications also survive; the originals are at TNA and records are also available on Findmypast. They may indicate that an ancestor at least intended to go abroad, but passports were not obligatory for travel outside the United Kingdom before 1914, and are unlikely to reveal an ancestor's destination. You may be able to locate your ancestor before his death using online overseas records, such as Ancestry's American and Canadian census records and passenger lists and, if you strike lucky, take the necessary steps to search for his death in the relevant country. Cyndislist.com has a very informative page on both death records and emigration records, which may help you track down useful online sources abroad.

Many UK deaths overseas were recorded and passed on to the respective British GROs. These are listed below, and the majority can be found on sites that offer the GRO index.

- British Forces abroad including deaths in the Boer War and both World Wars.

- British Consul or High Commissions in the country where they took place, from 1849. There was no obligation for the death of a British citizen to be registered by the Consulates or High Commission, so the returns are not complete. In some cases original consular records also survive and are held at TNA with online copies available at BMD Registers and TheGenealogist under their 'Non Parochial BMD' section. It is worth checking these too, as they may contain a small number of entries that did not make it to the GRO.

- Marine Deaths on British registered vessels from 1837 (1855 for Scotland and 1864 for Ireland). From 1874 all deaths were recorded by the Registrar General of Shipping and Seamen. The information was initially supplied by ships' captains but some information did not get sent on to the RGSS. Therefore it is worth looking at the original registers. BT 159 and BT 158, which cover 1854 to 1890 between them, are again online at BMD Registers and TheGenealogist, and BT 334 is on Findmypast. It is also worth looking at the registers for deaths collected by the Board of Customs from 1892–1918. These are to be found under CUST 67 and 74 and are more complete than their GRO equivalents.

- Aircraft Deaths, from 1948, which took place on British registered aircraft.

Some of the above are also indexed on Family Search in its 'Great Britain Deaths and Burials, 1778–1988' database. If you wish to find out exactly which countries are covered by the various databases held by TNA then they are all listed in *Tracing Your Ancestors in the National Archives* by Amanda Bevan (7th edn, TNA Books, 2006).

Extract from the registers of deaths at sea for 1878 compiled from ships' log books. (Image is Crown copyright BT 15845, reproduced courtesy of The National Archives and findmypast.co.uk)

For those people who died overseas or at sea, and who were resident in Scotland, the records for all but the last fifty years are available at ScotlandsPeople under its 'Minor records' collection. After this date you will need to apply for a certified copy of the entry. To search the minor records indexes you will need to select 'minor records' from the 'Counties/City/Minor Records' dropdown list found under the main 'Statutory Records/Deaths' search page. There are also extracts from registers for deceased seamen from Ireland, Orkney and Shetland, at http://freepages.genealogy.rootsweb.ancestry.com/~econnolly/register, while the Catholic registers on ScotlandsPeople also contain some overseas entries.

If an ancestor died in one of the British Colonies, then his death will be registered in the country where he died but *not* by the GRO up to the time that the country gained independence, or from 1949 onwards, whichever was sooner. In countries that had particularly close links with the UK, such as Australia, New Zealand and Canada, the Foreign Office did not take a record of British deaths even after independence, on the grounds that registration by the new governing authorities was deemed sufficient.

You may, of course, also be able to track down an ancestor via collections of burials relating to the British overseas (See Chapter 2). Deaths and burials in British India are held by the British Library in London and will be digitized by Findmypast in 2012. For further details see Emma Jolly's *Tracing Your British Indian Ancestors* (Pen and Sword, 2012). Family Search also offers records for many overseas countries, including some former British colonies, while the Society of Genealogists (SOG) has a good collection of overseas records including a fairly comprehensive set of indexes to Australian death records. They are listed under each individual state on the SOG library catalogue. London Metropolitan Archives (LMA) has a good information leaflet about BMDs overseas on its website, while Tim Yeo's book *The British Overseas: a guide to records of their births, baptisms, marriages, deaths and burials available in the United Kingdom* (3rd edn, Guildhall Library, 1994) is one of the most informative books in terms of which overseas records exist. If you know your ancestor died abroad, but his death was not registered by the UK authorities, then you will need to contact the civil registration authority for the country concerned.

Although the death certificates of serving soldiers in the World Wars can be a useful source for determining a soldier's rank, regiment and number, the cause of death will often only be described in general terms, such as 'killed in action'. More detailed information is usually to be found on the Commonwealth War Graves site (See Chapter 3).

Unknown Deaths

It is a sad fact that some people were never properly identified after death,

YOUNGER, George, 52...........Alnwick 10 b. 319
— Margaret Ann. 19.........S. Shields 10 a. 405
— Mary Ann. 33.........St. Geo. East 1 c. 233
— Mary Jane. 15.............Bourn 7 a. 989
YOUNGMAN, Jeremiah. 47.........Bury 8 c. 306
— Sidney James. ....Cambridge 3 b. 302
YOUNGS, Frances. 22 ....Wisbeach 3 b. 374
— George. 39.............Tendring 4 a. 187
— George Christopher. 63.........Gravesend 2 a. 257
— Henry. 78.............Blofield 4 b. 130
— Lucy. 73.............Blofield 4 b. 134
— Mary. 78.............Blofield 4 b. 133
— Ruth. 24.............Thetford 4 b. 269
— Samuel. 70.............Depwade 4 b. 143
— Walter. 0.............Islington 1 b. 167
— William. 73.............Loddon 4 b. 140
— Male. 0.............Dooking 4 b. 214
YOURN, James Henry. 2.........Bootle 10 b. 416
YOXALL, Elizabeth. 20.........Hexham 10 b. 172
YUILE, Albert. 1.............Warrington 8 c. 111
YUILL, James Patrick A. 2.........Holborn 1 b. 429
— Mary. 30.............Pancras 1 b. 79
YULE, Thomas Brisbane. 83.........Brentford 3 a. 68
— Male. 0.............Islington 1 b. 195

Z.

ZEALAND, Maria. 67.............Spilsby 7 a. 329
ZEALEY, Christabel Maria. 1...Marylebone 1 a. 393
ZECHBAUER, Male. 0.........Barton R. 6 a. 93
ZEPFERT, Charles Phineas. 1...Whitechapel 1 c. 172
ZERBE, Benton Hart. 39.....S. Shields 10 a. 387
ZERNISCH, Herman Frederick W. 1..Islington 1 b. 198
ZIEGER, Norman Ernest B. 1.......W. Ham 4 a. 60
ZIEGLER, Ella Sophie. 1 ....Chorlton 8 c. 429
ZILLWOOD, Thomas. 0.....St. Geo. H. Sq. 1 a. 252
ZOSSENHEIM, Sarah. 35.............Leeds 9 b. 338

U.

Unknown, Joseph. 0.............Leeds 9 b. 279
— Mary. 0.............Leeds 9 b. 314
— Richard. 58.............Newport, M. 11 a. 110
— Male. 0.............Pontardawe 11 a. 342
— Male. 5.............S. Shields 10 a. 435
— Male. 35.............Swansea 11 a. 402
— Male. 0.............Cardiff 11 a. 143
— Male. ....Newport, M. 11 a. 105
— Male. 60-70.........Pontypridd 11 a. 191
— Male. 25-35.........Chester le S. 10 a. 293
— Male. 0.............Mile End 1 c. 312
— Male. 50.............S. Shields 10 a. 441
— Male. 0.............Gateshead 10 a. 501
— Male. 0.............Newcastle T. 10 b. 53
— Male. 0.............Newcastle T. 10 b. 53
— Male. 26.............Rochdale 8 c. 61
— Male. 0.............St. Asaph 11 b. 263
— Male. 0.............Huddersfield 9 a. 271
— Male. 50.............Halifax 9 a. 315
— Male. 0.............Newcastle T. 10 b. 76
— Male. 0.............Newcastle T. 10 b. 20
— Male. 28.............Hackney 1 b. 307
— Male. 0.............St. Giles 1 b. 354
— Male. 40.............Poplar 1 c. 417
— Male. 50.............London C. 1 c. 7
— Male. 0.............Holborn 1 b. 402
— Male. 15.............London C. 1 c. 7
— Male. 0.............London C. 1 c. 33
— Male. —.............London C. 1 c. 8
— Male. 0.............Islington 1 b. 238
— Male. 50.............St. Giles 1 b. 343
— Male. 50-60.........Bristol 6 a. 10
— Male. 0.............Strand 1 b. 351
— Male. 60.............Hackney 1 b. 291
— Male. 0.............Hackney 1 b. 301
— Male. 50.............Pancras 1 b. 12
— Male. 0.............Holborn 1 b. 392
— Male. 35.............Thornbury 6 a. 133
— Male. 48.............Poplar 1 c. 404
— Male. 50.............Whitechapel 1 c. 210
— Male. 55.............Bridlington 9 d. 199
— Male. —.............York 9 d. 37
— Male. 45.............Bradford, Y. 9 b. 145
— Male. 80.............Bradford 8 d. 34
— Male. 30-35.........Prestwich 8 d. 224b
— Male. 50-60.........Salford 8 d. 58
— Male. 5.............Liverpool 8 b. 144
— Male. 25.............Oldham 8 e. 198
— Male. 0.............W. Derby 8 b. 425
— Male. 25.............W. Derby 8 b. 333
— Male. 30.............Liverpool 8 b. 81
— Male. 0.............Chorlton 8 c. 523
— Male. 45-50.........Ormskirk 8 b. 500
— Male. 0.............Ashton 8 d. 419
— Male. 0.............Salford 8 d. 32
— Male. 40.............Liverpool 8 b. 71
— Male. 0.............Chorlton 8 c. 469
— Male. 25-30.........Barton 8 c. 379
— Male. Adult.........Ormskirk 8 b. 502
— Male. 65.............Manchester 8 d. 172
— Male. 40.............Barton 8 c. 392
— Male. 0.............Salford 8 d. 20
— Male. 0.............W. Derby 8 b. 231
— Male. 0.............Edmonton 3 a. 117
— Male. 0.............Brentford 3 a. 29
— Male. 28.............Windsor 2 c. 265
— Male. 45.............Edmonton 3 a. 125

Unknown, Male. 28.............Bromford 3 b. 36
— Male. 0.............St. Alban's 3 a. 243
— Male. 0.............King's N. 6 a. 240
— Male. 0.............King's L. 3 b. 226
— Male. 30.............S. Stoneham 2 c. 33
— Male. —.............Runcorn 8 a. 153
— Male. 0.............Runcorn 8 a. 154
— Male. —.............Birkenhead 8 a. 340
— Male. 40.............Lambeth 1 d. 208
— Male. 40.............Greenwich 1 d. 515
— Male. 0.............Wandsworth 1 d. 351
— Male. 0.............Greenwich 1 d. 534
— Male. 0.............Wirral 8 a. 291
— Male. 0.............Wolverhampton 6 b. 368
— Male. 30.............St. Saviour 1 d. 3
— Male. 30.............St. Olave 1 d. 120
— Male. 40.............Leek 6 b. 192
— Male. 0.............Camberwell 1 d. 399
— Male. 0.............St. Olave 1 d. 118
— Male. 0.............St. Saviour 1 d. 89
— Male. 48.............St. Olave 1 d. 104
— Male. 0.............Aston 6 d. 148
— Male. 25.............Aston 6 d. 217
— Male. 22-23.........Solihull 6 d. 302
— Male. 60.............Bingham 7 b. 256
— Male. 52.............Derby 7 b. 295
— Male. 0.............Birmingham 6 d. 124
— Male. 0.............Falmouth 5 c. 125
— Male. 0.............Birmingham 6 d. 13
— Male. 60.............Bath 5 c. 443
— Male. 11.............Helston 5 c. 149
— Male. 0.............I. Wight 2 b. 378
— Male. 0.............Chelsea 1 a. 174
— Male. 20-60.........Romney M. 2 a. 549
— Male. 50.............Faversham 2 a. 451
— Male. 40.............Kingston 2 a. 190
— Male. 14.............Epsom 2 a. 21
— Male. 0.............Steyning 2 b. 178
— Male. 0.............Marylebone 1 a. 404
— Male. —.............Romney M. 2 a. 549
— Male. 0.............Bromley 2 a. 213
— Male. 0.............Steyning 2 b. 173
— Male. 45.............Rye 2 b. 6
— Male. 25.............St. Geo. H. Sq. 1 a. 293
— Male. 50.............Dover 2 a. 522
— Male. 35 to 40.......Luton 2 a. 260
— Male. 26.............St. Geo. H. Sq. 1 a. 292
— Male. 50.............Kingston 2 a. 190
— Male. 0.............Leeds 9 b. 256
— Female. 0.............Ulverston 8 c. 516
— Female. 0.............Poplar 1 c. 384
— Female. 0.............Atcham 6 a. 427
— Female. 0.............Islington 1 b. 147
— Female. 38.............Whitechapel 1 c. 210
— Female. 54.............Whitechapel 1 c. 210
— Female. 0.............Bethnal Green 1 c. 140
— Female. 33.............Whitechapel 1 c. 204
— Female. 40.............Shoreditch 1 c. 86
— Female. 0.............Islington 1 b. 20b
— Female. 0.............Islington 1 b. 232
— Female. 0.............Seaford 9 d. 218
— Female. —.............W. Ham 4 a. 71
— Female. —.............W. Ham 4 a. 70
— Female. 0.............York 9 d. 25
— Female. 0.............Bradford, Y. 9 b. 159
— Female. —.............W. Ham 4 a. 8
— Female. 0.............Holbeck 9 b. 209
— Female. 0.............Chorlton 8 c. 517
— Female. 0.............Oldham 8 d. 430
— Female. 0.............W. Derby 8 b. 412
— Female. 40.............Liverpool 8 b. 142
— Female. 25-30.........Prestwich 8 d. 297
— Female. 0.............W. Derby 8 b. 427
— Female. 0.............Liverpool 8 b. 119
— Female. 0.............W. Derby 8 b. 264
— Female. 0.............Liverpool 8 b. 106
— Female. 40.............Salford 8 d. 36
— Female. 0.............W. Derby 8 b. 264
— Female. 25-30.........Liverpool 8 b. 85
— Female. 0.............Liverpool 8 b. 129
— Female. 0.............Brentford 3 a. 59
— Female. 0.............St. Thomas 5 b. 38
— Female. 0.............S. Stoneham 2 c. 43
— Female. 0.............Brentford 3 a. 37
— Female. 0.............S. Stoneham 2 c. 38
— Female. 25.............Lewisham 1 d. 604
— Female. 0.............St. Saviour 1 d. 4
— Female. 0.............Wandsworth 1 d. 379
— Female. 50.............Lambeth 1 d. 207
— Female. 0.............Stoke T. 6 b. 126
— Female. 0.............Lewisham 1 d. 560
— Female. 40-50.........St. Olave 1 d. 157
— Female. 0.............W. Bromwich 6 b. 454
— Female. 25.............Lambeth 1 d. 209
— Female. 0.............Nottingham 7 b. 159
— Female. 35-40.........St. Geo. H. Sq. 1 a. 296
— Female. 45.............St. Geo. H. Sq. 1 a. 237
— Female. 0.............Kingston 2 a. 168
— Female. 0.............Richmond, S. 2 a. 207
— Female. 40.............Marylebone 1 a. 392
— Female. 0.............Kensington 1 a. 13
— Female. 50.............Kensington 1 a. 87
— Female. 45.............N. Aylesford 2 a. 266
— Female. 35.............Guildford 2 a. 59
— Female. 0.............St. Geo. H. Sq. 1 a. 231
— Female. —.............Westhampnett 2 b. 225
— Female. 0.............Westminster 1 a. 324
— Female. 0.............E. Preston 2 b. 219
— Female. 30-40.........St. Geo. H. Sq. 1 a. 277
— Female. 0.............Thanet 2 a. 490
— Female. 0.............Steyning 2 b. 171
— Unknown. —.............Wellingbro' 3 b. 80
— Unknown. 0.............Derby 7 b. 311

An extract from the 'unknown' section of the GRO index for the June quarter of 1880. (Image reproduced with the kind permission of findmypast.co.uk) and have been entered into the GRO index under the 'unknown' section. Although the number of entries can vary greatly in each quarter, Colin Rogers, in his book *The Family Tree Detective* (3rd edn, Manchester University Press, 1997), states that in 1840 about 500 unnamed corpses were registered. This gives an idea of the number of people whose lives you may never track down to their end. If a body could not be identified, then the entry will be entered in the appropriate quarter of the index, giving the sex, an approximate age if possible, and the registration district where it was found. Sometimes you will see entries where there is a first name but no surname, and one can only assume that the person in question lived on the streets and was known to locals by his or her first name. These listings come after the 'Z' section of the alphabet in the death index. If you have a good idea of when and where your ancestor died, then you can take a look to see if any entry of approximately the right age appears in a suitable district, but the results will almost always be inconclusive. The certificate will usually give details of where the body was found and there will have been an inquest. There may also be a short report in the local paper (See Chapter 5).

Aliases and Changes of Name

Some people are known by more than one name during the course of their life, and not just women who marry. If you fail to kill off one of your ances- tors then make sure you have checked that he did not marry or remarry before he died. Names were changed for other reasons too. Perhaps the person in question wanted a new start in life, maybe because they were running away from something, or someone. Perhaps he had married bigamously or had not remarried, but had deserted a spouse in order to live with someone else. Divorce was still only viable for the better-off classes up to the 1920s. No legal process was needed to change your name. Although you could make an announcement in a newspaper such as the *London, Edinburgh* or *Belfast Gazette,* you would obviously not do this if you wished to hide your past! It is almost impossible for a researcher today to find any trace of such a change. If the death was registered in the new iden- tity then you will not find it.

However, there may be clues to changes of identity. Many people appear to have been sentimental about their change of identity, choosing to keep their first name or adopting their mother's maiden name. If you suspect an ancestor did change his identity, then the only likely way to track down his death is firstly to try to locate someone of the same age and place of birth, with a likely surname, in the census returns and then look for his death. In most cases, however, it will be impossible to prove that the man who appears on that census return for which your ancestor does *not* appear, and who has the same first name, age and place of birth and perhaps the surname of his mother, might be your ancestor.

Where a name has been changed and the person in question was *not* hiding this fact he may appear under both his old and new name in GRO records. As we have seen, entries in the death index were based on information given by the person who registered the death. If this person stated that the deceased had had two names it is possible that an entry would be made under both names. In a 'missing relatives' case I worked on, all trace of my client's birth father petered out. This was because he had changed his surname! As chance would have it, he remarried in later life and, although his new surname was the main one under which he was entered on the certificate, his old name was also given. There were also two entries, one under each name, in the GRO marriage index. I was then able to locate his death, which was filed solely under his new name. If he had not remarried I would never have spotted his death entry as there was no ostensible connection between his old and new surname.

If you reach a point where you are faced with several possible certificates and you don't know which one relates to your ancestor, you will need to try and find out as much about your family as you can. Research into uncles, aunts, cousins and their children, as well as the immediate family, and from as wide a range of records as possible, may reveal new information that will narrow the time period in which your ancestor died and significantly reduce the number of possible certificates for you to buy. Your ancestor may, for example, be named as the executor in a relative's will, thus proving him to be alive at that point. Conducting further research may mean putting off buying the death certificate for some time, but may save much wasted money in buying certificates that do not relate to your ancestor. Burial entries can help narrow down a death in the GRO index before 1866 when no age was recorded. Ages were routinely given in burial records from 1813 and this, and the person's place of abode, may help narrow down the choice of certificates.

Apart from this, you will need to study your family on each census return, especially the last in which your ancestor appears. Note the address and compare this to your list of possible death entries, checking the civil registration reference aids already mentioned to see which area each registration district covered. It is also worth tracing all an ancestors' children in the census returns, to see in which part of the county they were living, in case your ancestor died there.

Locating and Ordering Irish Death Certificates.

Although Irish civil registration is very similar to that in England and Wales, there are significant differences in access. After the Partition of Ireland in 1921, a separate GRO was established for the north under the authority of a new Registrar General. To find out more about the history of the Irish General Registration system see the Irish General Register Office website www.groireland.ie/history.htm.

To buy death certificates relating to Northern Ireland up to the time of Partition you can apply to either the GRO in Belfast (GRONI) or Dublin (GROIRE). For deaths from 1922 onwards you will have to apply to GRONI. If you intend to search the registers yourself then both GRONI and GROIRE charge a fee. For full details of current charges and procedures relating to index searching, ordering certificates and what they include, see their respective websites at www.nidirect.gov.uk/gro and www.groire land.ie. Both also offer a search facility if you cannot visit in person. GRONI has recently announced plans to establish a website along what appear to be similar lines to ScotlandsPeople (see below) for viewing civil registration data. No further details are available at the time of writing.

For deaths in what is now the Republic of Ireland (the Irish Free State up to 1948) you must place your order via the GROIRE office in Roscommon, no matter when the death occurred. One advantage of the ordering system employed by GROIRE is that you are allowed to purchase a non-certified copy of an entry (a photocopy rather than a certificate), thus making it much cheaper. The other is that, since it includes records for the north before 1921, it is much cheaper to order uncertified copies from GROIRE rather than the obligatory certified, and much more expensive, copies from GRONI for this period.

Accessing the Irish GRO Index from Outside Ireland

The index is available online at Ancestry and via the Family Search website, but with limitations. Family Search has a database entitled *Ireland, Civil Registration Indexes, 1845–1958*; but this is misleading as it is not a complete index. Expert Irish genealogist Chris Paton, in his Scottish Genes blog of 14 April 2011 (http://scottishancestry.blogspot.com/2011/04), points out that, although the index covers the whole of Ireland up to Partition (with a few gaps in the third quarter of 1894), after this the database contains records predominantly for the Republic of Ireland. Although some entries for the north do appear after 1921, there is no indication as to what the actual coverage might be. The Ancestry database is also incomplete after 1921 (see the Scottish Genes blog for 21 September 2011 at http://scottishancestry.blogspot.co.uk/2011/09). If what you require is not available online, the complete index up to 1959 is available on microfilm from the Church of Latter Day Saints Family Search Centres or, of course, at GRONI. There are also copies of parts of the indexes created by local family history centres online at www.rootsireland.ie.

Death certificates in Ireland are similar to their English counterparts, the only difference being the addition of marital status in the Irish version. In the Republic of Ireland the names of parents are included from 2005 and this is soon to be introduced to Northern Ireland too. As in England and Wales, certificates ordered from the Irish GRO are duplicates of the original death entries registered locally. Many local registration offices will allow access to their locally held records, while the Church of Latter Day Saints has microfilmed copies of the original registers for 1864–70 for all Ireland and 1922–59 for Northern Ireland. These can also be ordered from Family Search Centres on microfilm.

For finding out more about addresses on Irish certificates look at www.irishhistoricmaps.ie for Republic of Ireland Historic Ordnance Survey maps and https://maps.osni.gov.uk/mapconsolehistorical maps.asp for Northern Irish OS maps. Many trade directories for Northern Ireland are available at www.proni.gov.uk.

Locating and Ordering Scottish Death Certificates

The Scottish certificate gives far greater detail than its counterparts elsewhere in the UK, including the time of death and marital status. Most importantly, however, it includes the name and occupation of the deceased's parents (also noting if they were deceased by this time), and the name of any spouses (although this was not recorded between 1856 and 1860). Burial details and the name of the undertaker were also given between 1855 and 1860. Entries recorded in the initial year of civil registration only also note the deceased's birthplace and names of any children, together with their ages or dates of death where applicable.

The amount of detail given in Scottish entries means it is easier to identify the correct entry; a problem so often encountered in English, Welsh and Irish entries. They are not infallible, however: a problem commonly encountered is that the person registering the death gave inaccurate information, sometimes listing the parents' names incorrectly.

The death of Angus McGugan in 1859 shows how much information was required compared to registration elsewhere in the UK. (Reproduced with the kind permission of the Registrar General for Scotland)

The Scottish death index lists the deceased's date of birth from 1967 and the mother's maiden name from 1974, while married women are indexed under both their maiden and married names.

Although the Scottish system of civil registration followed the English version in its overall format and organization, there are some significant differences in terms of how to locate and obtain copies of them. Perhaps the biggest is that you can view entries of death (and births and marriages) *without* buying a certificate. With the exception of entries under fifty years old, all are available online at ScotlandsPeople, listed under 'Statutory Records'. The site works on a pay-per-view basis. Those deaths not yet online can be seen either at the ScotlandsPeople Centre in Edinburgh or the Glasgow Genealogy Centre at the Mitchell Library. Alternatively, you can pay for a search to be done at local registry offices, followed by the issuing of a certified copy of the entry. If you cannot get to Edinburgh or Glasgow yourself, a better option is often to hire a local genealogist to search for you. Scottish death entries have been filmed directly from the original death registers that were kept at local level and are thus less prone to copying errors. Ages at death were not routinely included in the index until 1865, although these are gradually being added to the online index.

Incorrect Scottish Entries

The Register of Corrected Entries or RCE (renamed the Register of Corrections in 1965) records any amendments made to Scottish entries of death (and birth and marriage). Any amendments were written into the register and the original entry annotated to show this. If such an annotation appears when researching online via Scotlandspeople, you can click on the amendment to view the extra information. The register cannot be searched independently. RCEs for deaths also include the results of precognitions from the Procurator Fiscal's Office, following sudden or accidental deaths. These are the equivalent of a coroner's inquest in England and Wales.

The inclusion of the parents' names on Scottish death entries often helps identify the birth or baptismal entry for your ancestors, so it pays to search for it at an early stage. Once you have located it, you have a head start over your English counterparts, because you will know the names of the previous generation of the family. This comes with the aforementioned rejoinder that the details provided by the informant may not always be accurate. For investigation into addresses on Scottish death records the National Library of Scotland has a wonderful collection of Ordnance Survey and other maps available online at http://maps.nls.uk.

The Channel Islands and the Isle of Man

The Channel Islands and the Isle of Man are dependencies of the Crown and, as such, have their own governments and administrative systems. The Channel Islands are divided into the two Bailiwicks of Jersey and Guernsey, with civil registration of deaths beginning in Guernsey in 1840, in Jersey in 1842, in Alderney in 1850 and Sark in 1915. Many of the records will be in French.

The death registers for Jersey are not open to inspection, although both the Channel Islands Family History Society (www.jerseyfamilyhistory .org), and La Societé Jersiaise, have copies of the death index between 1842 and 1900, and undertake research on behalf of the general public for a fee. Otherwise, applications for certificates (which currently cost £20 each) must be made to: The Superintendent Registrar, 10 Royal Square, St Helier, Jersey JE2 4WA. Before you do this it is worth looking at both www.societe-jersiaise.org and www.jerseyfamilyhistory.org/research, which provide a good introduction and useful advice for potential researchers.

On Guernsey both the death index and the registers themselves are available for public inspection at HM Greffier, The Royal Court House, St Peter Port, Guernsey GY1 2PB (they keep records for Sark as well) and also at the Priaulx Library in St Peter Port. Their website at www.priaulx library.co.uk provides a good introduction to tracing your Guernsey family history. Married women will be recorded in the death index under their maiden name up to 1949, while many deaths were not registered, even after the introduction of civil registration. In this case you may have to search for a burial instead. The Society of Genealogists in London also has copies of the Guernsey death index up to 1963.

Enquiries concerning deaths on Alderney should be made to The Greffier, Registry for Births, Deaths, Companies, Land and Marriages, St Anne, Alderney GY9 3AA.

Compulsory civil registration only began on the Isle of Man in 1878, so before this date you should look for burials instead. Copies of death certificates can be obtained from the Douglas Civil Registry, Deemsters Walk, Bucks Road, Douglas, Isle of Man, IM1 3AR or, if you are visiting the island, the original registers may be viewed; but check opening times before you visit. SOG has a copy of the death index up to 1964.

Chapter 2

BURIAL RECORDS

Burial records may form part of the parish registers of the Church of England (also known as the 'Anglican Church'), the registers of nonconformist (non-Anglican) churches, or relate to burials in civil cemeteries. Just like death certificates it is easy to overlook burial records in our haste to trace our family tree backwards in time, yet they have an important role to play in both pre- and post-1837 research. Not only do they provide an approximate date of death but, if an age is given, this can help in the search for your ancestor's baptism. Knowing your ancestor's lifespan will help you identify him in other local records such as the parish poor rate or quarter sessions, while burials may lead you to gravestones and corresponding memorial inscriptions containing details about your ancestor's life. You may occasionally be delighted to find that an entry for your ancestor contains anecdotal evidence about him which will not be found anywhere else and, occasionally, you will find children buried whose baptisms were simply not recorded.

Case Study: Using a Burial to Help Trace a Baptism

Despite finding a baptism for my ancestor John Perdue in Goudhurst, Kent, in 1802, I could find no trace of his parents, John and Ann, in the area before this date. Since there were no census records at this time, I had no idea of how many other children they had, which would have indicated an approximate date for their marriage and, in turn, their own baptisms. They could have been married at any point in the twenty-five year period before the birth of their son in 1802 while, based on his mother's likely age at his birth, her baptism could have taken place between 1757, when she would have been 45, and 1788 when she would have been 14. I did find burials for John and Ann in Goudhurst in 1855 and 1848 respectively, however, and these gave their ages and showed that John was born in around 1756 and Ann in around 1777. Even allowing for some inaccuracy in the burial entries, this substantially narrowed down the period of time in which I needed to search for their marriage and respective baptisms.

Parish Registers in England and Wales

Parish registers record the details of baptisms, marriages and burials conducted in the Church of England (this included Wales). They potentially range in date from 1538 up to the present day. In 1538 Henry VIII's minister, Thomas Cromwell, issued an injunction stating that, henceforth, the church should keep records of all baptisms, marriages and burials carried out in each parish. Although similar systems were introduced in countries such as France and Spain at about this time, Cromwell's injunction was met with a great deal of suspicion and resistance from clergymen and the public alike. There was already much unrest in the country caused by Henry VIII's controversial decision to sever ties with the Catholic Church, deny the authority of the Pope and make the English monarch head of the newly formed 'Church of England'. It is hard for us today to appreciate how shocking this was for the people of the time. Many clergymen felt that the monarch was robbing the church of its power and that he had no right to do so. Rumours spread like wildfire, claiming that there was to be a new charge for baptisms, marriages and burials. Some of the clergy encouraged these rumours. In fact, what Cromwell had actually said was that there would be a fine if the entries were *not recorded*. Public opinion was against him, however, and as a result very few parish clergy obeyed the injunction. This is the reason why few parish registers begin in 1538. Some events were recorded, but many were lost within a relatively short space of time because they were written in poor-quality paper books or on loose sheets of paper.

It was only with the growing stability of the reign of Queen Elizabeth (1558–1601) that parish registers were completed on a regular basis. In 1598 new legislation ordered that each parish should purchase parchment registers, which were more durable than the old paper books. Entries prior to this were to be copied out into the new books as well. This was good because it means that we have a record of many pre-1598 entries but, because the early entries were copies, they were inevitably prone to transcription errors. The other downside of the new legislation was its wording, which stated that copies of earlier entries should be made 'especially from the first year of her Majesty's reign'. The majority of clergymen and clerks naturally took the easy option and began their copies from the start of the Queen's reign in 1558, ignoring any earlier entries.

The 1598 legislation also ordered that copies of all new entries should be made and sent to the bishop annually. These are known as the 'Bishops' Transcripts' and, although few complete sets survive, they can provide a vital back up where the original parish registers are missing. Occasionally, whoever made these copies added or corrected details as he went along, so it is worth checking them against the originals if you suspect an error in the latter. You may also find 'Archdeacons' Transcripts', which were similar copies sent to the Archdeacon.

Early Burial Entries 1538–1812

The layout and amount of detail to be found within parish registers has changed over the centuries. There was no set format to early registers and the way of organizing them and their neatness was left to whoever completed them. This was usually the clergyman, the parish clerk or sometimes the churchwarden – but for simplicity we shall refer to him as 'the clergyman'. Although early burial entries are vital for compiling pedigrees, using them can sometimes prove to be a frustrating experience! Many comprise part of what are known as 'composite registers'. This is where the register has been completed as events occurred and baptisms, marriages and burials were not separated out into different books. Sometimes an attempt was made to segregate events within the register by setting aside a certain number of pages for baptisms, marriages and burials respectively, but when these had been filled the clergyman had to skip to the next free page (which might have been two or twenty pages away) to start a new batch of burials. Sometimes the clergyman would make the decision to enter burials at the back of the book, turning it upside down and working inwards from the back cover. This means it is not always easy to locate the next batch of burials, especially if viewing the records on microfilm. In 1754 new legislation meant that marriages had to be recorded in a separate book, but most parishes continued to record baptisms and burials in the same register up to the end of 1812.

An attempt to improve the quality of parish registers was made by the government in 1711 when it determined that the pages of the registers should consist of ruled lines and all pages should be numbered; but this had very little effect.

Very early burial entries can be frustratingly lacking in detail, often simply recording the person's name. Although there is a tendency for parish registers in general to contain greater detail from the seventeenth century onwards, burial entries vary greatly from parish to parish and can remain succinct, to say the least, until the nineteenth century. Where there is more than one person with the same name in the family, or living in the area at the same time, it can thus be hard to determine who the entry relates to. In 1645 a new Act of Parliament stated that burial entries should include the date of death, but this had little impact because it was passed during the chaos of the Civil War.

This extract from the parish register of 1561 for Holy Trinity the Less, City of London, shows how early entries of baptisms, marriages and burials were frequently entered chronologically rather than by type of event. (Copyright © Ancestry.com. All Rights Reserved)

Case Study: Helps and Hindrances in an Early Burial Register

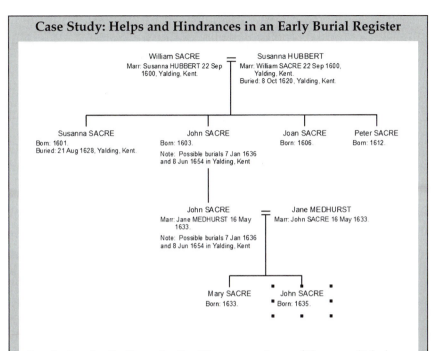

Family tree for the Sacre family. The recurrent use of the name 'John' made it difficult to identify burials with certainty. (Author's collection)

While reconstructing a seventeenth-century pedigree for the Sacre family of Yalding in Kent, the lack of detail in the burial register[1], combined with the repeated use of the forename 'John' in the family, proved a hindrance. I found burials for a 'John Sacre, householder' in both January 1636 and June 1654, but was unable to identify which of the two adults with this name each referred to.

Similarly there were burials for three different 'Susan Sacres' in 1599, 1620 and 1628. Thankfully some of these entries had a little more detail. The name 'Susanna' is interchangeable with 'Susan' and I had a lady on the family tree called Susanna Hubbert. She had married William Sacre in 1600 and had a daughter called Susanna, baptized in 1601.

The 1628 entry definitely referred to the daughter as it supplied her father's name. The entry for 1620 read: 'Suzan Sacry the wife of William of East Peckham together with her unbaptized son.' So this was highly likely to be Susanna Hubbert, and indicated that William and Susan had moved from Yalding to the nearby parish of East Peckham. This accounted for the fact that there were no further entries for the family in Yalding after the 1620s, apart from a possible death for William in 1631. He may have chosen to be buried back in Yalding alongside his wife. The third burial was for 'Suzan Sacry a single woman', buried in 1599. She must belong to an earlier generation of the family.

There are exceptions to the rule however. Some burial registers routinely included the cause of death, such as that for St Giles Cripplegate in the City of London in the 1660s, which also lists occupations. This makes especially interesting reading as it covers the time of the Great Plague of London.

In others parishes some clergymen seemed to relish adding extra details about late parishioners! The following are taken from the collections at Kent History and Library Centre. The first entry is dated 1705 and effectively provides the deceased's dates of birth and death. The clergyman's comment at the end shows that he thought the dates of her birth and burial were worth reporting.

The burial register for St Giles Cripplegate for August 1665 shows the devastating effect that the plague had on the City that year. The remaining two causes of death in this extract were recorded as 'Teeth' and 'Convulsions'. (Copyright © Ancestry.com. All Rights Reserved)

Maria Lownde widow 80 years. She was born on Christmas Day dyed on Good Fryday and buryed on Easter day. Remarkable.

If the death were tragic then full details may be included, such as this entry from Brenchley in Kent in August 1669.

Buried the 13th day of this month George Large, Broadweaver, and Matthew Weeks, his wife's son, a youth. Both which were stricken dead together in their own dwelling house by that dreadfull Tempest of Thunder and Lightning the evening before. From Lightning and Tempest, and sudden death, Good Lord deliver us.

In some cases the clergyman provides his own opinion or interpretation of what has passed and this may give us an insight into prevailing attitudes of the time. Another example from Brenchley brings home to the modern researcher just how suicide was regarded in this entry from 1670.

Buried the 6th of this month by the highway side at the five wents Mary the wife of Stephen Dawson, who wretchedly hanged herselfe in her owne house the 4th daye. The Good Lord preserve us from such satanicall Temptations and actions and help us to live and die in thy fear.

If you are lucky your ancestors may have lived in a parish that has what are known as 'Dade registers'. These are registers where the entries contain significantly more detail than normal, and they were the idea of the Revd William Dade. They are to be found from the 1760s up to 1812 and are concentrated in Lancashire, Yorkshire, Nottinghamshire and Durham. In 1798 the Revd Shute Barrington, Bishop of Durham, ordered that a similar, though slightly less detailed system, be used throughout the Diocese of Durham. This again continued up to the introduction of new-style registers in 1812. Although the entries most affected were marriage and baptism entries, burials will usually include the date of death, cause of death and sometimes the name of one or more parents, even when the burial refers to an adult. This entry is from Addingham in West Yorkshire:

Susannah Fentiman wife of William Fentiman of Addingham, butcher. Died Aug. 28th. Buried Aug 29th of this year [1799] 26 years, Child bed.[2]

Up to the end of the sixteenth century many parish registers will be in Latin, but don't let this put you off. By the time you get back this far in your research you will be familiar with the simple terminology used in burial registers, and it should not be too difficult to interpret the Latin with the help of a book such as Janet Morris's *A Latin Glossary for Family and Local Historians* (FFHS, 2002). In many cases the clergyman who wrote out the register often only had basic Latin himself, and you will find that some registers are a hotchpotch of English and Latin. Although some Christian names are easily recognizable to a researcher with no Latin, some are not. William, for example, is written as *'Gulielmus'* and the endings of the name may change depending on its role in a sentence. What may prove more difficult is the style of handwriting (palaeography), which can make it hard to interpret surnames. Spelling in pre-eighteenth century documents can vary tremendously and the same word may even be spelled differently in one document. Surnames in particular were prone to variant spellings even into the late nineteenth century.

Learning to read documents in different styles of handwriting is a skill that must be learned, but there are many useful books on the subject. TNA has excellent beginners' palaeography and Latin tutorials on its website; the latter includes a useful vocabulary. If you are looking for one surname in particular you will find that you soon learn to recognize it no matter the style of handwriting, while many sixteenth and seventeenth century hands prove easier to read than later counterparts. From 1733 English became the language for all official documents.

Change of Calendar

Before 1 January 1752 England and Wales used what is known as the 'Julian calendar'. This calendar calculated time based on how long the earth takes to orbit the sun. New Year was considered to begin in the spring when the centre of the sun was crossing the equator. The first day of the calendar year was designated as 25 March. If you are not aware of this then a child who, for example, was baptized on 2 April 1745 and buried on 2 January 1745 will appear to have been buried before he was baptized!

Like many calendars, the Julian calendar did not take into account the fact that the time the earth takes to orbit the sun is not consistent, and not easily divisible into exact units as required by a calendar. By 1751 the Julian calendar was actually eleven days ahead of 'real time'. Many European countries and also Scotland had already changed to the Gregorian calendar, which coped with the irregularity of the earth's orbit by using leap years. In 1751 the English government decided that the Gregorian calendar should be adopted instead. Although the New Year of 1751 began, as usual, on 25 March, it ended on 31 December and the first day of 1752 began on 1 January. Eleven days were omitted from September 1752 to correct the slippage that had occurred under the old system.

Where pre-1752 records have been transcribed or recorded after the event you may see what is known as 'double dating' for events taking place between 1 January and 24 March. So a burial that took place on 3 January

1745, for example, may be written as 3 January 1745/1746. This shows that when the event occurred the year was 1745 but, according to the modern calendar, it would have been 1746.

The Civil War and Commonwealth Gap

The English Civil Wars (often referred to as the 'Civil War') and the ensuing Commonwealth period lasted from 1642 up to the restoration of the monarchy in 1660. This period often causes problems for researchers because there are many gaps in parish registers at this time. These were initially caused by the ejection of many local clergymen from their parishes, leaving no-one to keep the registers. In 1653 Oliver Cromwell's government took away control of parish registers from the local clergy altogether. A new civil officer known as 'The Parish Register' was to be elected by local ratepayers and take charge of recording entries of birth, marriage and death (note death not burials). He was supposed to start new books in which to record these events, but in many cases the old parish registers were still used, while burials rather than deaths were often still recorded. Where separate civil registration books were created, very few survive. With the return of the monarchy in 1660 burial entries in parish registers resumed as before.

Burial Entries from 1813

An Act of Parliament in 1812, often referred to as 'George Rose's Act', set out new mandatory criteria for the completion of burial entries, meaning that burial entries from 1813 onwards look very different to their predecessors. Entries were now recorded into ruled books containing sections for the required information. This included the following: full name, age, place of residence, occupation, date of burial and the name of the person performing the service.

Searching for burials from this date onwards is much easier because of the regimented layout of the registers, but it means there are far fewer entries where extra information has been added. Occasionally, however, a post-1813 burial entry will include a comment such as that for the burial of Daniel Stiff in 1813 in Norton St Andrew, Suffolk, who was 'thrice married and was followed to the grave by about 150 of his relatives or descendants'[3] or the burial in 1862 of Stephen and Harriet Booth, aged six months, in Benenden, Kent, where a footnote states:

> Two of 3 children born at one birth. Buried in one coffin. Her Majesty the Queen sent the mother, after their birth, a present of Three Pounds, as is her usual custom in such cases.[4]

Name.	Abode.	When buried.	Age.	By whom the Ceremony was performed.
George Wilson No. 81.	Brenzett.	Feby. 3	weeks 11	R Warrener
Sarah Ann Sevenoaks the illegitimate daughter of No. 82. Jane Masters	Ivychurch	March 8th	months 6	R: Warrener
Joseph Tolhurst No. 83.	Ivychurch	July 5	yrs 7	R. Warrener
Ann Mackley No. 84.	Ivychurch	July	yrs 54	R Warrener

BURIALS in the Parish of Ivychurch in the County of Kent in the Year 1829

An extract from the burial register of Ivychurch, Kent, for 1829. Notwithstanding the regimented layout of post-1812 burial registers, some vicars still added extra details. (By kind permission of Ivychurch PCC)

Annotations in Burial Entries

As you trace your family in the burial records you may notice various annotations alongside some of the entries, which can be baffling to the layman. The one that most often puzzles researchers is 'buried in wool'. In 1666 the government passed an Act of Parliament stating that all bodies had to be buried in a woollen shroud. This was an attempt to boost the English woollen trade. In 1678 further legislation insisted that an affidavit had to be sworn by the relatives (or those responsible for burying the deceased), confirming that the body had indeed been buried in wool. The affidavit could be signed either by a JP, or the clergyman. There was a hefty

Hawkshead, in Cumbria, is one of the few parishes for which the original affidavits for burials in wool survive. These can provide details of the deceased's relatives. (Cumbria Archive Centre Kendal WPR 83 A79 file 1 Burial in Woollen certificates 1680-1696)

fine levied on the family and clergyman for failure to comply, and so burial entries would often be annotated to show that the body had been buried in wool or that an affidavit had been signed. Paupers were exempt from the regulations.

A few parishes have surviving collections of affidavits and these can provide details of the deceased's relatives. Some parishes also kept a book listing affidavits received. Although the Burial in Woollen Acts were not repealed until 1814, they were increasingly ignored from 1750 onwards and all but defunct by 1780.

In 1694 the government introduced a tax of four shillings on burial entries, along with similar taxes on birth and marriage entries, in order to raise funds for the war against France. Paupers and their families were again exempt. You may see the letter 'P' (pauper) written by the side of the entry. It is believed that sometimes an obliging vicar could be persuaded to mark the entry with a 'P' in order for a family to avoid the tax! The account books of the Overseers of the Poor, the parish officials who were in charge of handing out poor relief, are another potential source for the burial of paupers. Where these account books survive, they will often record instances where the parish paid for the burial of a poor person, usually recording the person's name and cost of the burial. These will be in local record offices.

In early burial registers you may find the use of the term 'chrisomer'. A chrisomer was a child who died within a month of its baptism. The chrisom cloth was a white robe used during the baptism ceremony, which the baby traditionally wore for a few weeks afterwards. If a child died as a chrisomer, the cloth would also be used as his shroud. In some places this term was used to indicate an unbaptized child.

If you see the term 'mort' next to a burial entry this refers to the medieval custom whereby the parish clergyman was entitled to a parishioner's second best beast (or later a monetary payment in lieu) after his death. This continued in some parishes into the eighteenth century, but only applied to the more wealthy parishioners. Such an annotation next to an entry indicates that payment was made.

Locating Burial Entries

The majority of burial registers are kept at county record offices or their equivalent. Here the originals are stored, while access is given to the public on microfilm. The record office may also have printed transcriptions of burials for some parishes. A growing number of burials are available online, either as transcripts or as digital images. Ancestry has a large collection of London and West Yorkshire burials while Findmypast, TheGenealogist and Familyrelatives also have growing collections from around the country. Some county record offices such as Essex and Medway have digitized and put some of their parish registers online too, while a search engine may reveal online transcriptions made by individuals. GENUKI lists many online transcriptions in its 'Church Records' listings and if you are lucky your parish may be the subject of a 'One Place Study', where a dedicated volunteer has transcribed not only parish registers, but also many other records. Current One Place Studies are listed at www.one-place-studies.org. A similar scheme known as 'Online Parish Clerks' also offers a selection of online burial transcriptions, and details can be found at www.onlineparishclerks.org.uk.

Many valuable transcriptions have been published over the years by societies such as the Lancashire Parish Register Society, the Harleian Society and also the Parish Register Transcription Society, which offers its publications online and on CD. The original books are often available in academic libraries. Many such transcriptions now form part of the online parish register databases of the major commercial genealogy websites. The Society of Genealogists (SOG) has a wonderful collection of parish register transcriptions, while the Institute of Heraldic and Genealogical Studies

(IHGS) has a useful collection in its library at Canterbury and both have online catalogues. The Church of Latter Day Saints has many local Family Search Centres dotted around the country as well as a massive record office in London where you can order copies of parish registers on microfilm. Their site at www.familysearch.org has a growing collection of transcriptions and images of burial registers available for no charge. Any transcripts should be checked in the original records where possible, not just to rule out any copying errors, but because there may be extra information in the original entry.

Many family history societies also publish parish registers on CD and you can find a list of them at www.ffhs.org.uk, the website of the Federation of Family History Societies.

There is no comprehensive index of burials and your ancestor's parish of residence is likely to be the best place to look. Your research will usually have provided you with this information, but if you fail to find what you are looking for, there are several methods of attack for you to pursue.

Missing Burials

Many ancestors did not stay put in one parish, and you will need to investigate burials of neighbouring churches too. There are many maps and parish listings available online or for sale that will help you organize your search and determine which churches existed in the area at a certain time. GENUKI offers a wide range of online maps depicting parish boundaries, while the IHGS sells parish maps for each county, available by post or in its shop. These are also reproduced in *Phillimore's Atlas and Index to Parish Registers*, edited by Cecil Humphery-Smith (Phillimore, 2003), which includes a full listing of all parishes in England, Wales and Scotland and the dates of deposited registers. All record offices will have county maps showing parish boundaries, while some also offer these online.

These maps will help you determine which other burial registers to search first. You may decide to search any relevant online burial databases before you make a visit to the record office. This is sensible, but make sure you make an ordered search for the burial, noting all parishes you have checked. It is easy to forget what you have looked at and what you haven't when working online. Ensure you have looked in all neighbouring parishes for the burial, even if you find a possible entry online further away. You may find there is another burial of someone with the same name in a parish much nearer to home.

The National Burial Index (NBI) is an incomplete but growing collection of burial records derived from parish, nonconformist, Roman Catholic, Quaker and cemetery records in England and Wales, and this may lead you to the missing burial. The current edition contains over eighteen million records and is available at Findmypast or on CD from the

Federation of Family History Societies, where you can also view a coverage chart indicating the percentage coverage for your county of interest.

The most comprehensive listing of parish registers is probably the National Index of Parish Registers, which is in several volumes and can be bought on a county by county basis from SOG. It also lists Catholic and nonconformist registers.

Your research may well show that your ancestor lived within walking distance of more than one church, so it pays to check these first. Unlike events such as baptisms or marriages, you will usually find the burial has taken place within a reasonable distance of where he died: after all, no one wants to cart a coffin further than necessary! Studying an Ordnance Survey map of the relevant date (they are generally available from the early 1800s), and bearing in mind what transport options there would have been at the time, may rule out some churchyards because the only available route was particularly tortuous.

If you fail to find the burial in the vicinity, the usual explanation is that your ancestor moved away from the family's home parish, often to live with a grown-up son or daughter. Further research into his children, using parish registers, the IGI on Family Search (see 'Tips for Research' at the beginning of the book) and census returns from 1841 onwards will often identify where they were living. If you suspect that your ancestor may have travelled abroad SOG has many collections of overseas burials and memorial inscriptions. (See Chapter 3 for a listing of websites offering overseas data.) It's also a good idea to search any available databases for what are called 'monumental inscriptions'. These are records of the inscriptions on gravestones and will indicate the place of burial. We shall look at these in the next chapter.

Some burial entries were simply not recorded through the negligence of the clergyman. In times of epidemic when many people were dying it was hard to keep track of who had died. In some cases the person who completed the burial register was himself taken ill and many entries were therefore not completed. Other registers have been lost or stolen. In this case look for alternative sources such as surviving Bishops' Transcripts or even churchwardens' account books, which sometimes record burial details alongside any fees paid to the church. The parish registers for Kendal have a very frustrating gap between 1631 and 1679 where the registers have 'disappeared', while the corresponding Bishops' Transcripts only survive for three of these years. However, there are surviving churchwardens' accounts dated 1669-1734 that note all burials conducted, the name of the person, the date and the fee paid to the church.

A small percentage of missing burials can be accounted for by the fact that there was no legal requirement for a person to be buried in a churchyard. Prisoners may have been buried within the prison complex, while a small minority died at sea (see Chapter 1) and some people, usually

Quakers, were buried in gardens or orchards. If your ancestor served in the army or navy then both the Royal Greenwich Hospital and the Royal Chelsea Hospital for navy and army personnel respectively had their own burial grounds. The records for the latter will be found at TNA in RG 4 together with many nonconformist registers (as mentioned below) while those for the Greenwich Hospital are at TNA under ADM 73. The Royal Hospital for army pensioners at Kilmainham in Ireland also had adjoining burial grounds for officers and non-commissioned officers.

Nonconformist and Catholic Burial Records

Even if you believe your family to have been staunch members of the Church of England it is likely that some of them will have become members of a nonconformist church, if only briefly. The term 'nonconformist' refers to protestant churches that set up independently, or broke away entirely, from the established Church of England from the 1660s onwards. It includes the Society of Friends (Quakers), Presbyterians, Methodists, Baptists and Congregationalists as well as many other groups, some of which were very short-lived. Few nonconformist churches (with the exception of the Quakers) had their own burial grounds until the 1800s, and before this most nonconformists would have been buried in the parish churchyard.

Every Christian (apart from convicted felons), had the right to burial in the local churchyard as long as he had been baptized, no matter whether or not he was a member of the Church of England when he died. The vicar was also obliged to perform a service during the burial unless the person was excommunicate or had committed suicide. In some burial registers you may see the annotation 'Anabaptist', or in the case of a Catholic burial, 'papist' or 'recusant' alongside an entry. The Anabaptists were an extreme sect of religious reformers, but this word was often used in this context to simply denote the burial of any nonconformist.

Unlike nonconformists, who could be buried wherever they liked, by law all Catholics had to be buried in the parish churchyard together with an accompanying Church of England service up to 1844. They were only officially allowed to establish their own burial grounds from 1852, although a few had opened before this. Michael Gandy has written two books entitled *Catholic Missions and Registers 1700–1880* in six volumes (M. Gandy, 1993), and *Catholic Parishes in England, Wales, Scotland and Ireland; An Atlas* (pub. M. Gandy), which will help immensely with research in this area.

The Burial Laws Amendment Act of 1880 meant that for the first time burials could take place in consecrated ground (so in a Church of England churchyard) *without* the performance of a Church of England service, as long as the person burying the body informed the vicar of this fact at least forty-eight hours in advance. This led the way for nonconformists to be buried in parish churchyards using their own ministers and own form of worship, if they wished. The act also enabled Church of England clergy to perform a burial service in unconsecrated ground. Two years later a further act allowed suicides to be buried in the churchyard with a religious service, which they had previously been denied, although this had to take place between nine at night and midnight.

Quaker Burials

If your ancestors were Quakers you can revel in the extremely detailed records of deaths and burials that they kept (usually combined in one entry), although they rarely erected headstones until the mid-nineteenth century and, before the opening of their own burial grounds, they often favoured burial in gardens or orchards. Their burial records may date back as early as 1656. Early records usually include at least the date of death, and date and place of burial and may give the cause of death too. In 1776 they introduced printed books in which the name, date of death, age, residence, occupation and place of burial were recorded. The information would be recorded twice, once by the local Quaker 'Preparative meeting' and once by the local 'Quarterly meeting'. The Quakers refused to use the standard names for the days and months because some were derived from the names of pagan gods. Therefore you will see them referred to sequentially in the registers. September, for example, was thus the 'seventh month', although when the calendar changed in 1752 it became the ninth month. For further information on the Quakers read *My Ancestors Were Quakers* by Edward Milligan and Malcolm Thomas (SOG, 1999)

When Died.	Name.	Age.	Refidence.	Defcription.	When Buried.	Where Buried.
26 /11... 1806	George Saunderson	76	Kendal	Clogger	28 /11... 1806	Kendal.
6 of 1... 1807	Ruth Hoggarth	78	Crook	Widow	11 of 1... 1807	Crook.
10 of 1... 1807	Ann Hopkinson	70	Kendal	Widow	18 of 1... 1807	Kendal.
10 of 2... 1807	Hannah Spend	80	Kendal	Widow	23 of 2...1807	Kendal.
3 of 3... 1807	Job Field	70	Kendal	. . . .	6 of 3...1807	Kendal.
18 of 3... 1807	Thomas Simpson	11	Plumbgarths	Son of Joseph & Hannah Simpson	23 of 3...1807	Kendal.

Extract from the Register of Burials for the Quaker Monthly Meeting of Kendal, Westmorland from 1805–06. (© Crown Copyright. Images reproduced by courtesy of The National Archives, London, England. www.NationalArchives. gov.uk & www.TheGenealogist.co.uk TNA Reference RG6 / Piece 874 / Folio 0)

Locating Nonconformist Burial Grounds

There are several excellent guides to the records of the various non-conformist churches published by SOG and they provide listings of surviving records (see Bibliography). Nonconformism was especially popular in Wales and a useful guide to surviving registers is Dafydd Ifans's *Nonconformist Register of Wales* (Aberystwyth: National Library of Wales and Welsh County Archivists' Group 1994). Both the previously mentioned *Phillimore's Atlas and Index of Parish Registers* and *The National Index of Parish Registers* include Catholic, Jewish and nonconformist records. GENUKI also has some useful links to information about these records.

Some nonconformist churches, such as the Methodists, were organized on a circuit basis under the charge of one minister. He was responsible for a large area and moved around holding services at different locations. In this case there would be just one set of registers for the whole circuit and you will need to check the books mentioned above to discover which circuit covered the area where your ancestor lived. Many nonconformist records have not survived because the minister would often carry the register with him on his rounds, and also take it with him when he left the district.

The majority of nonconformist records for England and Wales are now available online, which to a large extent reduces the need for so much homework! The Non-Parochial Registers Act of 1840 required all non-conformist groups to submit any registers they held. Although a few of these were rejected by the GRO because they were poor quality, most are held at TNA under RG 4-6, while RG 8 includes registers handed in after a further request by the government in 1857. These include some Catholic records and records of the Russian Orthodox Church in London. Digital images are available at BMD Registers and TheGenealogist. These websites also give access to burial records of British citizens abroad and deaths on British ships (RG 32). It is also worth checking with the local record office and any libraries connected with each religious group to see if any of the rejected registers have been deposited there, but these are only a minute number. SOG holds transcripts of many nonconformist registers.

Few nonconformist registers survive before the eighteenth century but, if your ancestors came from London or its vicinity, it is worth checking the records of Bunhill Fields Cemetery mentioned later in this chapter.

Jewish Burials

Although few Jewish UK burial records survive before the eighteenth century, those that do are available on Family Search. There are many Jewish burial grounds in London and other parts of the United Kingdom.

One of the earliest Jewish burial grounds in London was the Old Mile End burial ground which was operating from 1657 until about 1720. After this date a new burial ground opened further along the road. Records of the new cemetery are available at Ancestry and at www.jewishgen.org/databases/UK, which also lists many Jewish burials from cemeteries around the UK. Those of the Old Mile End cemetery are in volume nineteen of the *Transactions of the Jewish Historical Society*, copies of which can be found at academic libraries or second hand. Where there was no local Jewish burial ground, many municipal cemeteries would set aside areas for Jewish burials, while it is worth looking at www.cemeteryscribes.com which provides details of Jewish gravestones in the United Kingdom. Dr Antony Joseph's *My Ancestors Were Jewish* (4th edition, Family History Partnership, 2008) is a useful guide to tracking down Jewish death and burial records.

Cemeteries and Burial Grounds

From the 1850s onwards there was a rapid growth in the development of cemeteries serving both urban and, later, rural areas. One of the main reasons for this was the increasing lack of space in churchyards, especially in large towns and cities. Cemeteries or burial grounds (the latter term often referred to a burial place for a particular denomination) were not just a nineteenth-century phenomenon, however, and were popular with nonconformists, most of whom preferred not to be buried in the parish churchyard because it was consecrated ground. With the exception of the Methodists, most nonconformist groups considered the consecration of land for burial to be unnecessary and superstitious. Bunhill Fields in London was established in 1665 for nonconformist burials and proved to be immensely popular, with an estimated 120,000 people buried between 1665 and 1852.[5] The burial registers only survive from 1715 and are at TNA, while a number of memorial inscriptions with photographs are available at www.findagrave.com. Similarly Ballast Hills Cemetery in Newcastle also buried nonconformists and opened in 1609, although the registers only begin in 1792.

Despite these early examples, public cemeteries that buried people of all faiths or denominations did not really evolve until the nineteenth century, when private companies ran them as profit-making businesses. The first of this kind was 'The Rosary' in Norwich, established in 1819. The cemetery at Kensal Green, which opened in 1833, was the first in London. This followed the government's decision to grant licenses to several private companies to build cemeteries that would serve the capital's growing population. London's churchyards had become unhealthy places of putrefaction, largely because there was insufficient room left in them, while the first outbreak of cholera in the city in the early 1830s exacerbated the problem.

Further legislation in 1852 prevented any new burials in London church-yards, although some took place where an old grave was reopened for a family member. It also gave parishes throughout the country the authority to establish cemeteries or burial grounds away from the parish church, if there was the need. Thus you may find that some rural areas have burial grounds some distance from the parish churchyard. These were initially under the control of burial boards (groups of elected parishioners), but in 1894 control was transferred to the newly-formed local government authorities. From the 1850s onwards your city-dwelling ancestors are most likely to have been buried in a municipal cemetery.

Cremation was very much a development of the twentieth century and was illegal until 1884. The church argued that it prohibited the physical resurrection of the body, and it took a challenge in court to legalize it. The first crematorium opened in Hull in 1901, but it was not until the Second World War that it became increasingly popular.

Locating Burials in Cemeteries

There are several online databases listing burials in cemeteries, and there is a large crossover with sites listing information from gravestones. I have listed these in Chapter 3. General information about individual cemeteries is available via the internet so ensure that you check the opening date for the cemetery. There is no point in searching for a burial which occurred before a cemetery opened!

Getting the Most from Burial Entries

We have seen how causes of death may be given in burial registers, but even where they are not, careful observation of the register may show a particularly high proportion of burials over a certain period. This may indi-cate that the local population had been the victim of an epidemic. There are many internet sites that list known historic occurrences of epidemics. Improving your knowledge in this area may help shed light on the possible cause of your ancestor's demise, or point to his survival in a time when much of his village was affected. If your ancestors lived in London during the 1660s you may well be struck by the staggeringly high number of deaths caused by the plague that was at its height in 1665.

Burial registers may contain other notes made by clergymen at the time, or added at a later date. Studying the parish registers for your ancestor's town or village can provide a wonderful insight into what life was like at the time. Many clergymen also added extra notes to the registers regarding events that occurred in the parish. The burial register for Benenden, Kent, contains several pages that record full details of many gravestones within the church that were soon to be permanently covered over by the restoration work undertaken between 1861 and 1862. During my research I have also seen references to murders, freak weather conditions, and comments on a person's character. One entry for an elderly woman alluded to the fact that she had been deserted many years previously by her husband and it was not known whether she was a wife or a widow!

Make sure you use all your sources in conjunction with each other. A study of monumental inscriptions and burials in conjunction with baptism records may show that there are baptisms missing from the parish registers and therefore from your family tree. You may occasionally find that your ancestors had children whose baptisms and burials have gone unrecorded in burial registers, although their short lives are commemorated on a gravestone. Monumental inscriptions often give far greater detail about the deceased compared to the burial entry and we shall look at these in the next chapter.

Case study: William and Charlotte Heritage. Further Research from a Burial Entry

My ancestors William and Charlotte Heritage were married in 1782 in Stratford upon Avon. Like many people they did not remain in one parish. By 1787, when their son Charles was baptized, they were living a few miles south of Stratford in the village of Ettington, and it was there that four of their eight children were buried; the last in 1796. In 1799 William took out a lease on nearby Whichford Mill, but eighteen months later an auction notice in the local paper showed him putting many of his goods up for sale prior to leaving the mill for good. Then the trail went cold.

I was unable to locate a burial for either William or Charlotte in the vicinity of Whichford or Ettington, but identified two possible entries at Haselor, a village a few miles north of Stratford. The first was for a William Heritage buried on 29 November 1818, aged sixty-eight, and the second for a Charlotte Heritage buried on 29 June 1831, aged sixty-nine, and also at Haselor. As far as I was aware, however, neither had any connection with Haselor, which is about twelve miles away from Ettington. No gravestone survived to indicate that they were buried together and prove that they were husband and wife. 'Heritage', although not a common name, is heavily localized in the area and I knew that my William had several namesakes. I therefore needed further evidence to prove that I had found the correct entries.

I noticed that the burial entry for Charlotte described her as 'of Redditch', and this provided me with a vital clue. If she was living at Redditch, but buried at Haselor, it was probable that she had previously lived at Haselor but had moved away after William died in 1818, perhaps to live with a son or daughter. When William had died

---

60

Haselor churchyard in Warwickshire where William and Charlotte Heritage were buried. (Author's collection)

Charlotte had probably invested in a double grave plot so that she could be buried with him when her time came. Although Redditch is over the county border in Worcestershire, it is only about twelve miles away from Haselor. In order to see if I could find further evidence to support my theory I looked for evidence that any of Charlotte's children were living in the Redditch area. I knew that her son Charles, my direct ancestor, was not and so I considered her other children: William, Esther and Thomas. My first move was to see if there were any children baptized in the Redditch parish registers that might be Charlotte's grandchildren. A search revealed baptisms for a Charlotte, Ellen, Caroline and Betsey Heritage between 1820 and 1826 to parents Thomas and Mary Heritage, and a marriage for Thomas and Mary in 1817. In the light of this it seems highly likely that I had found the correct burial entries and that, after William died in 1818, Charlotte moved in with Thomas and Mary. When their first child was born in 1820 they named her after her grandmother. If Thomas and Mary had not been baptizing their own children at this time it would have been more difficult to prove my theory. In that case I could have used other sources, such as local tax records or trade directories, which might have pinpointed Thomas living in Redditch. Confirming that these were the correct burial entries was very important as it was the only indication of the year of birth for both William and Charlotte, which proved vital in the search for their baptisms.

Burials in Scotland

Scottish burial entries are sparse in number compared to their English and Welsh counterparts because there was no legal requirement for such records to be kept. Some may note the date of death and others the date of burial. The earliest records date to the start of the seventeenth century, but these early entries are relatively rare, while in many parishes the recording of burials was intermittent. There was also a tendency for people to be buried in the parishes of their ancestors rather than where they themselves had lived. Married women were usually referred to by their maiden name, although their husband's name was usually included too.

An alternative source is the recording of payments for use of the parish mortcloth, which was the cloth used to cover the coffin en route to burial. These may be found either in the parish registers or in the kirk sessions. The fee for its hire was often waived for the poor, who will therefore not be recorded.

Scottish parish records are to be found at the ScotlandsPeople Centre in Edinburgh and in selected local record offices, but all are available via the Scotlandspeople website, which also lists each parish and the years for which burial entries survive. Similarly it also holds Catholic and non-conformist burial records and entries made in the 'Register of Neglected Entries' (RNE). The RNE register was compiled by the Scottish Registrar General after the introduction of statutory registration in 1855. It contains entries of deaths (and births and marriages) proved to have occurred in Scotland between 1801 and 1854 but never entered into the parish registers.

Irish Burial Registers

Survival rates and the locations of Irish burial records vary according to whether they belonged to the Church of Ireland or the Catholic Church. Fewer than half of all Catholic parishes kept burial registers before 1900 and earlier registers were often only kept on an intermittent basis. There tend to be a greater number of surviving registers in the north of the country, while the sparsest coverage is to be found in rural areas.

By contrast, burial registers for the Church of Ireland started much earlier. The majority begin between the 1770s and 1820s, but in some urban areas they may date back to the 1630s. They usually include the name, age and townland and an estimated third of parishes have surviving records. Although some are still held in the original parishes many are available on microfilm, either at the National Archives in Dublin, or at the Library of the Church of Ireland Representative Church Body (RCB). Both publish a list of parishes whose records they hold on their respective websites. The Public Records Act of 1867 declared all parish registers before 1870 to be subject to general public access and required them to be deposited at the National Archives of Ireland unless adequate facilities for storage could be provided by the parish. Sadly nearly all of these were lost in the fire at the record office in 1922. The records that survive today are mainly those that had not been deposited and consist of over 600 registers. *A Table of Church of Ireland Parochial Records and Copies* by Noel Reid (Irish Family History Society, Naas, 1994) will indicate whether or not burial registers survive for a particular parish.

Although the original Catholic burial registers remain with the parish priest, many have been microfilmed and are available at the National Library of Ireland up to 1880, with a few going up to 1900. Further information and a listing of what is available can be found at www.nli.ie/en/parish-register.aspx.

The Public Record Office of Northern Ireland holds all surviving copies of Church of Ireland registers for Northern Ireland, with some filmed copies held locally. For a full listing of what is available there is an online guide to church records at www.proni.gov.uk.

Further information about Irish church records can be found at www.progenealogists.com/ireland/churchrecords.htm and www.irish-times.com/ancestor/index.htm.

Chapter 3

GRAVESTONES AND MONUMENTAL INSCRIPTIONS

Mankind has used stones to commemorate the dead for centuries. Some of the earliest stones, which commemorated high-status members of society, date back to Anglo-Saxon times. For standard genealogical purposes, however, you are unlikely to find any surviving gravestones before the seventeenth century, while time and air pollution has rendered many of these illegible. It is a sad fact that, although our ancestors may have spent a tidy sum erecting a stone to a much-loved family member, only those made of slate, or situated in a sheltered location, will have survived in good condition. Many stones of less durable material have totally crumbled away. Frederick Burgess, in his book *English Churchyard Memorials* (Lutterworth Press, 1963), surmises that the use of memorials for the middle classes would have been the norm by the end of the fourteenth century, but these memorials were probably made of wood and did not survive for long. The number of surviving seventeenth-century memorials made of stone indicates that, as a material for memorials, it was affordable for the middle classes by this time. It was not until the late eighteenth and early nineteenth century that gravestones became affordable for the majority of the population, however. This was as a result of an improved transport network that in turn reduced the cost of stone. Even so, the burial plots of poorer families would remain unmarked by any stone right into the early twentieth century.

Traditionally, the favoured place for burials was on the south side of the churchyard, the northern side being associated with evil spirits and often reserved for the burial of strangers or the poor. In older churches you may notice that the ground on the south side is far higher than that on the north, and this is usually because the great number of burials there has elevated the ground level. More important parishioners will usually be found buried or commemorated inside the church and these memorials, barring destruction as a result of church renovations, will usually have survived in excellent condition.

What Will the Stones Tell You?

Gravestones are an excellent source for dates of death and birth although, like any other source, they are not always accurate. Information given to the stonemason may have been incorrect, while just like the print setter in the newspaper or the clerk who wrote out death certificates, stonemasons did occasionally make mistakes. I have seen several stones where dates have clearly been altered by the mason, although in many cases I suspect mistakes were not rectified!

Finding a gravestone can be an alternative way of tracking down a death certificate or a burial entry, while the age at death will indicate a person's approximate year of birth and help you identify your ancestor's baptism correctly. Since many burial entries before 1813 do not provide this information the gravestone can be vital evidence in this respect.

Gravestones are excellent sources for providing details of other family members too and it is always a good idea to note the names of families in adjoining plots, even if they have different surnames. During my initial

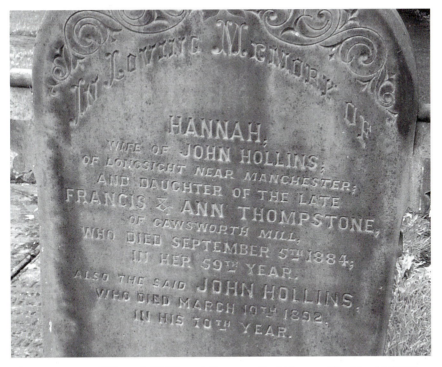

The gravestone of Hannah Hollins at Gawsworth, St James, Cheshire (d.1884), which gives the name and place of residence for both her and her parents. (Author's collection)

Banff, St Mary, Aberdeenshire. This stone in memory of the infant children of James Harper and his wife Katharine Philips gives James's occupation as 'shoemaker' while, like most Scottish memorials, it also records the mother's maiden name. (Author's collection)

exploration of Aston Cantlow church in Warwickshire, where my Heritage family was buried, I noted the stones of those people surrounding them. Many bore the surname 'Clements' and it turned out that they were related to another branch of my family tree; so my notes stood me in good stead for the next stage of my research. Gravestones will often help flesh out existing information on your family tree; they may tell of a second spouse, infant children who died, or even other family members such as nephews, nieces and grandchildren. Occasionally you may find a gravestone for someone who fails to appear in the burial register, probably because the

Richmond, St Mary, Yorkshire. Gravestones that record a cause of death, such as this one for Agnes Atkinson who died of child bed in 1812, are particularly helpful before the introduction of death certificates. (Author's collection)

entry was accidentally omitted from the register. You may also find details of grown-up children, some of whom were added to their parents' gravestone even though they had left home and married. This was often the case if they had died soon after marriage, perhaps without having children of their own. In the case of a woman this will give you her married name and, although there may be no direct descendants, this is all part of building a picture of your family as a whole. If you are looking for gravestones of women in Scotland, women are usually recorded under their maiden names but with a reference to their husband's name too.

If you are lucky your family memorial may provide extra information in the form of the deceased's occupation, place of birth, residence, or how he died; the latter is extremely welcome before the advent of death certificates in 1837. Occasionally you may find reference to someone's personality or to the esteem in which they were held. The stone for Margaret Seguin, who died in 1883 at Brabourne in Kent, reads, 'the only sister of Jane wife of William D'Ombrain of Canterbury to whose family she was much endeared. God loveth a cheerful giver'. Bearing in mind that most stonemasons charged by the word there is some truth in saying that only better-off families could afford a lengthy inscription, but it only takes a few extra words to give you an insight into a person's character or a vital clue as to

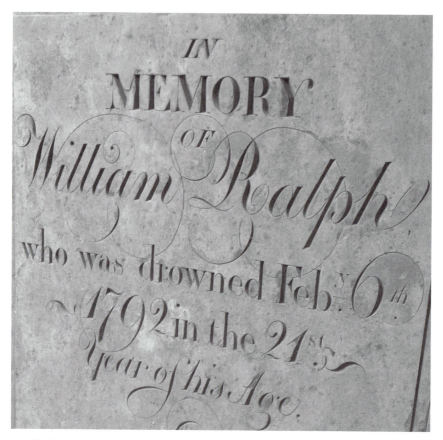

Deaths by drowning, such as that of William Ralph who drowned in 1792 aged twenty-one, were a common occurrence in coastal parishes where many parishioners went to sea, or where unfortunate strangers were washed up on the shore. Church of St Martin-in-Meneage, Cornwall. (Author's collection)

where he originated from. By contrast the stone for James Johnston in the churchyard of Orphir in Orkney not only lists places and dates of birth and death for his immediate family, but also lists all his ancestors back to the sixteenth century with their dates too – truly a family historian's dream come true!

Artwork on Gravestones

Although the written words on our ancestors' graves are of greatest importance, it is also worthwhile considering any accompanying artwork. Many stones are completely unadorned: although this would often have come

Richmond, St Mary, Yorkshire. Gravestones frequently tell a tale of numerous infant deaths. Your ancestor may not have grown up with the bevy of siblings you imagined from looking at the baptism register. The Cowling family lost three children, but many families lost an even greater proportion of their offspring to infant death. (Author's collection)

down to cost, other factors such as fashion and the preferences or ability of the local stonemason also play a part in determining the artwork on a grave.

Take a close look at any imagery on your ancestors' memorials. Much was symbolic and can sometimes give an insight into aspects of your

Case Study: The Gravestone of Margaret Clements

Finding a gravestone, or its transcription, can save time searching other records for deaths, births or baptisms. Stephen Clements married Margaret Harding in 1899 and they had four children in the next five years before Stephen was tragically killed in a carriage accident. A newspaper report gave full details of his death and burial and I easily located his grave in Aston Cantlow churchyard. Next to it was Margaret's grave. Her stone told me that, despite being only twenty-eight when Stephen died, she remained a widow until her own death fifty-eight years later in 1962. Today, with many transcriptions available online, gravestones are increasingly becoming a quick and easy short cut for identifying a date of death and helping to locate the correct death certificate; this is especially useful where there is more than one possible death in the GRO index. Margaret's stone also indirectly told me that she must have brought up her four young children by herself.

Aston Cantlow church with Clements' graves in foreground. (Author's collection)

ancestor's life or character. A wheat sheaf, for example, was an indication of a full and contented life, representing a good harvest, while a thistle represented hardship or sin. Occasionally the tools of your ancestor's trade may be depicted on the stone: a weaver, for example, might be indicated by a loom or shuttle. Certain other symbols were more run of the mill, such as the book and the trumpet, both of which represented eternal life, or a hand emerging from a cloud, representing God's presence. The hourglass and the skull and crossbones or 'death's head' represented man's mortality and the passing of time. These are often found on gravestones up to the late eighteenth century, and their depiction on many seventeenth-century stones can be extremely simplistic. Some stonemasons clearly struggled with such images, resulting in rather cartoon-like images which may cause amusement today! If, however, you find a well-carved skull and cross-bones that has weathered the centuries well, it presents an arresting and often gruesome sight.

Rather than studying your ancestor's stone in isolation, take a look at others of a similar era in the churchyard and neighbouring churchyards.

The urn was a popular feature of gravestone ornamentation in the late eighteenth and early nineteenth centuries. Church of St Michael and All Angels, Penkridge, Staffordshire. (Author's collection)

71

Skull and crossbones or death heads were frequently depicted on pre-nineteenth-century gravestones, but the way in which they were carved by the local stonemason varied greatly. This one on the head of the stone for William Calloway, dated 1784 (St Clement, Cornwall) appears almost humorous to modern eyes. By contrast, that on the stone of Alexander Long, dated 1723, (St Laurence, Ramsgate, Kent) is fairly gruesome. (Author's collection)

This stone from Banff, St Mary, Aberdeenshire is an extravaganza of symbols representing mortality and eternity and includes a cherub (winged soul), trumpet, arrow of death, hour glass, coffin, and skull and crossbones. (Author's collection)

This will help you determine whether the images and decoration on your ancestor's stone are the result of a special request by the family, possibly to reflect that person's life or qualities, or part of the local trend in monumental artwork at the time. The numbers of monumental masons working in one area would not have been large and you will often see the same themes and styles repeated throughout graveyards in the same region. You may also spot the mason's name on the back or at the bottom of a stone.

Memorials inside a Church

Much of the finer detail of the artwork on stones in churchyards has been lost, but studying the imagery on the memorials inside the church often gives us an idea of what they would have looked like in their prime. Images on the stones outside would often have mimicked that found on the grand tombs inside the church. Internal memorials can provide a wealth of infor-

Meanings of Symbols on Gravestones

These are just a few of the symbols you may come across. See the Bibliography for further reading on the subject.

Images representing mortality, the brevity of life and inevitability of death:

- Pickaxe and spade: the tools used to dig a grave
- Butterfly – was thought to mate and die in a day
- Death's head or skull and crossbones
- Hourglass
- Lighted candle (conveyed the passing of time or the fragility of life i.e. when the candled was snuffed)
- Urn
- Coffin
- Dart, arrow, javelin or scythe – traditional way of representing death's deadly blow

Images representing resurrection or eternal life:

- Angel (sometimes lifting a coffin lid)
- Winged cherubs (often used to represent the soul with wings leaving the body)
- Sunrays and clouds
- Trumpet
- A book (representing the Book of Life where the names of all who were destined for heaven were written.) It could also be used to represent the Bible, or a learned person)
- Serpent with tail in its mouth (thus creating a circle and representing eternity)

mation about more prominent parishioners and you may be able to build up a detailed family tree simply from reading through them. Many will relate to armigerous families (those entitled to bear heraldic arms). In this case they will usually display the family coat of arms (properly called an 'achievement of arms') and show how these evolved with each marriage. If you have an understanding of heraldry a lot can be learned about the deceased's pedigree by reading the coat of arms. There is not space here to define the rudiments of doing so, but *Discovering Heraldry* by Jacqueline Fearn (Discovering Books, 2006) is a good introduction, as is Stephen Friar's *Basic Heraldry* (A & C Black Ltd, 1999). Much information can also be discovered about such families via the internet.

While you are exploring inside the church don't just look for tombs; you may also find memorials in windows, such as that at Gawsworth church

This memorial to the Tilden family of Ifield Court, Northfleet, provides details of four generations of the family. (Author's collection)

in Cheshire to 'Fred Trueman of the 10th Cheshire's who died for his country in France 30 March 1916'. Plaques may commemorate the establishment of charitable trusts made when someone died. Thus we find in Oddington in Leicestershire the following plaque:

> Joseph Harvey late of Churchill in the County of Oxford gave by his Will dated January 25th 1812 to the Rector and Churchwardens of this parish and their Successors £100 upon trust, to place the same out at Interest, and to distribute the Interest to the Poor of this Parish on Saint Thomas's day forever.

Locating Gravestones

At the point you start looking for your ancestors' gravestones you will often have carried out a significant amount of research into your family history and you may already have located their burial record. Alternatively, you may stop to explore a church because you believe your ancestors came from the area, having done little supporting research beforehand. In the early days of my own research (long before records went online) I would take any opportunity to visit a parish where I knew my ancestors had lived if I was in the area, often without having had the opportunity to look at the burial register or many other sources beforehand. Although not a methodical approach, there was a great element of excitement and expectation in exploring the churchyard like this. The thrill of finding several family graves over the years far outweighed the many other occasions when my Mum and I spent much time, often in the pouring rain, traipsing around a churchyard only to find nothing!

It is, however, beneficial to work in a more methodical fashion and there is another source you can use to locate your ancestors' gravestones more easily. These are known as 'monumental' or 'memorial inscriptions' (MIs) and are transcriptions of the writing on gravestones. While this may not give you the same thrill as actually seeing your ancestor's gravestone, many were compiled in the nineteenth and early twentieth centuries and captured the wording on stones that are now illegible or do not survive. Today there is a steadily growing number of online databases that offer information about both monumental inscriptions and burials. Naturally, finding an MI will lead to the burial place and corresponding entry in the parish registers, and finding the burial may lead you to the gravestone and/or monumental inscription, so it helps to search the various databases in conjunction with each other.

Record offices will hold copies of local monumental inscriptions, while many family history societies have published their own transcriptions too. Check their websites to see what they offer for sale. The Federation of Family History Societies website at www.ffhs.org.uk provides a list of societies. The Society of Genealogists has a good collection of MIs from all over the United Kingdom, and overseas. You can check what they have via their online catalogue. If you do make a visit to the church where you believe your ancestor is buried, it is worth venturing inside before you start hunting in the graveyard in case there is a list or plan of who is buried where. If you find no stone or monumental inscription for your ancestor, despite knowing he was buried there, remember that the number of burials in a churchyard is usually far greater than the number of stones that survive. Stones did not just erode, but were also recycled; there are instances of both wooden and stone memorials being reused for later burials or sometimes as building materials! In the Home Counties, until relatively recently, many memorials were constructed of wood and these were particularly prone to decay.

Traditionally, locating the burial of an ancestor who lived in a large town or city and who was likely to have been buried in a cemetery could be difficult since most had large catchment areas. Cemetery databases could only be searched individually and many cemeteries also charged a fee for searches. Things have become a lot easier thanks to the recent flood of online databases listings both burials, cremations and memorial inscriptions.

If the entry you are seeking is not in any online database there are many listings available both in print and online to help you pinpoint likely cemeteries. An internet search will often bring up a list of all cemeteries under local authority control, together with details of how to apply for a search of the records, and opening times. A very useful finding aid for London is *Greater London Cemeteries and Crematoria* by Clifford Webb and Pat Wolfston (3rd edition SOG, 1994). Certain London cemeteries tended to cater for particular localities of the city, while some, such as Brookwood in Surrey, offered cheaper burials and, as a result, buried many of the poor from the East End of London. This guide will help point you in the right direction.

Websites for Monumental Inscriptions and Burials

The sites below all contain information relating to burials, monumental inscriptions or gravestones. Most are work in progress, and while most have a UK bias some have a preponderance of American or Canadian records which may help trace ancestors who emigrated. Some are free, while some require payment for downloading information. Many burial entries are also, of course, included in the parish register collections of the major commercial genealogy websites such as Ancestry and Findmypast.

- www.worldburialindex.com

Thousands of inscriptions and images from gravestones in the UK and overseas.

- www.gravestonephotos.com (The Gravestone Photographic Project)

Free site. Aims to place online details and images of all gravestones before 1901.

- www.billiongraves.com

Records and some images from cemeteries across the world, although the bias is heavily American.

- www.deceasedonline.com

Central database of statutory burial and cremation registers for the UK and Republic of Ireland. Not yet complete but covers many UK cemeteries and crematoria and very helpful for London research.

- The National Burial Index is available at www.findmypast.com as part of its 'Parish Records Collection'.

- www.findagrave.com

Details and images of gravestones in cemeteries from around the world

---

- Ancestorsatrest.com

Mainly graves from USA and Canada but a number of Irish cemeteries are covered and a few from England and Scotland.

- www.canadianheadstones.com

Canadian Headstone Photo Project

Free site. Contains records of some 300,000 records of gravestones in Canada and these are also indexed on Ancestry.

- www.namesinstone.com

Free site offering Canadian and American gravestone details. It includes an estimated 900,000 records.

- www.nmm.ac.uk/memorials

The National Maritime Museum Memorial Index. Transcriptions of monuments commemorating British people with maritime related work or careers and the victims of disaster at sea.

- http://kentarchaeology.org.uk

Kent Archaeological Society. Wonderful collection of nineteenth-century Kent churchyard inscriptions.

- www.bacsa.org.uk

The British Association for Cemeteries in South Asia. Lists many British cemeteries and isolated graves and memorials in South Asia.

- http://glosgen.co.uk/index.htm

Lists war memorials and some church memorials in Gloucestershire.

- www.jewishgen.org/databases/UK

Incorporates the JewishGen Online Worldwide Burial Registry with 1.7 million names.

RG 8 at TNA (see Chapter 2) includes registers of burials in the Victoria Park Cemetery, the New Burial Ground, Southwark, Bunhill Fields Burial Ground, Hackney, the Bethnal Green Protestant Dissenters Burying Ground and the Russian Orthodox Church in London.

Once you have located the cemetery, if you wish to visit the grave, it is wise to contact cemetary staff to obtain its exact location. Cemeteries are divided into sections and each grave has a number, which the cemetery should be able to supply, often together with a plan to help you locate it. In some cases they may also provide you with information from the grave books which detail exactly who was buried in each grave. You may find other family members who are not mentioned on the gravestone, or in some cases your ancestor may be buried in a grave with several other unrelated people; these are often referred to as 'pauper' graves because the family could not afford a private grave. These will rarely have any headstone. Despite the fact that my great-grandparents Mary and James Wilson were relatively comfortably off for most of their lives, when Mary died in

1928 she was buried in a pauper's grave in the cemetery at Whitton, Middlesex. The cemetery staff gave me the names of the other five people buried there (all unrelated) and marked the plot so I could find it.

Older cemetery records are often housed in the local archives and may include not only burial registers, but also plans of the cemetery showing grave numbers. These can be particularly helpful in locating a grave if you already have a grave number from a memorial card (see Chapter 7).

War Graves and Memorials

If you are looking for the grave of an ancestor who died as a serviceman or woman in either the First or Second World War, your first point of call should be the Commonwealth War Graves Commission website at www.cwgc.org. Originally called the Imperial War Graves Commission, but renamed in 1960, the commission was founded in 1917 and commemorates all who died during the First and Second World Wars in

The Nine Elms Depot war memorial at Waterloo Station commemorates the employees of the Southern Railway's Nine Elms Motive Power Depot who died in the Second World War and is just one of many war memorials in and around the station. (Author's collection)

service, or of causes attributable to service. It maintains military cemeteries across the world and you can search for your ancestor in its database. The database includes not only those whose bodies were recovered and who have individual graves, but also those soldiers whose bodies were never identified. The National War Memorial website at http://ukniwm.org.uk is a growing compilation of all United Kingdom war memorials which also has a searchable online database.

My uncle Ronald Heritage died at sea while a Prisoner of War in 1944 and his body was never recovered. Although he has no grave, he is commemorated on the wall of Kranji cemetery in Singapore. His entry on the Commonwealth War Graves Commission website gave me details of his parents, his wife and her address, his date of death and the location of his memorial in the cemetery. It also provided his service number (very useful for potentially identifying him in other records), his rank, the name of his regiment and battalion number.

Case Study: Elizabeth Heritage: A Gravestone rediscovered!

My great-grandparents Charles Chapman Heritage and Elizabeth Clements married in 1812 at Aston Cantlow in Warwickshire. The parish registers showed that they had five children before Elizabeth died in 1822 aged thirty-three. I discovered Charles's gravestone in the churchyard many years ago and this told me that after Elizabeth's death he married her sister! Sadly, Elizabeth's stone did not survive. I struck lucky, however, and during a visit to Warwick Record office discovered the 'Aston Cantlow Parish Scrapbook', which had been compiled by the local vicar in the mid- to late 1800s. As part of the book, he had not only transcribed all the gravestones in the church-yard, but had also made detailed sketches of them. This included Elizabeth's stone and by the sketch was a note stating 'this stone is no longer in existence 1869'. The drawing provided me with details not only about Elizabeth, but also three children who had died as infants. Two of these, Charles and Elizabeth, are to be found in the burial register, but the third, Ann, was not recorded in either the baptism or burial registers, and appears in no other parish's registers either. The sketch indicates simply that she 'died in infancy'; it is probably the only trace of her existence. Interestingly, it also shows that baby Charles died aged five, although the parish registers show he was only two years old when he died. This must have been either a transcrip-tion error in the book, or a mistake on the original gravestone. Both the memorial inscriptions and the burial entry provided information about Elizabeth's age at death and therefore her year of birth, which in turn helped me to identify her baptism and that of her sister Margaret, Charles's second wife, in a parish in Worcestershire.

The sketch of Elizabeth Heritage's gravestone in the Aston Cantlow Parish Scrapbook. (Warwickshire Record Office DR0259/68/1–42)

Chapter 4

INQUEST RECORDS

If your ancestor was unlucky enough to die an unexpected or violent death, there is often an opportunity to learn much more about him using inquest records. In an age before the advent of welfare benefits, effective painkillers, counselling, credit cards and the Health and Safety Executive a shocking number of people met their end in accidents or at their own hands. Take a look through a local paper from the mid- to late nineteenth century and you will see what I mean! Your ancestor's death does not have to have been violent to be the subject of an inquest, however. Any death that was simply unexpected would also be reported to the coroner, who would, in many cases, hold an inquest to determine the cause and circumstances of the deaths reported to him. He was also responsible for investigating any deaths that occurred in jails and other institutions such as workhouses and asylums.

Although, on the face of it, the coverage dates for inquest records are impressive, ranging from the fourteenth to the twentieth century, there are certain limitations that can make them frustrating records to use. Survival rates are extremely patchy and, although this is remedied from the nineteenth century onwards by good newspaper coverage, comparatively few newspapers are yet indexed. The average family historian will only be able to trace his family tree back to the sixteenth century at best, so inquest records before this time are rarely of direct use to him, while records before 1733 are in Latin and therefore difficult for most people to interpret. Early inquest records may be of use, however, if the surname being researched is rare. In this case, they can act as evidence for locating the name in a certain area at a particular time, which may help identify its evolution and migration. Inquest records really come into their own from the mid-nineteenth century once they can be used in tandem with death certificates and newspaper reports.

The Coroner and the Jury

The office of the coroner was officially established in 1194, although inquests previously took place under the authority of various different officials. Over the centuries, although procedures and the amount of medical evidence provided have changed, the basic investigation he makes remains remarkably similar. His name derives from the word 'corona' which means 'of the crown' and indicates that, although originally elected by local freeholders and later county councillors, a coroner was, and still is, working on behalf of the crown. Originally his primary role was a fiscal one, it being his job to investigate any matters that could potentially bring in crown revenue. The reason that this included investigating sudden deaths was because various fines were payable to the monarch in many such cases. After the Norman invasion in 1066 a system developed whereby the local Anglo-Saxon community was liable for a hefty fine if any Norman was found to have been murdered. A body was presumed to be Norman unless it could be proven otherwise! The early coroners spent much time dealing with this sort of business while, until 1846, any object that caused the accidental death of a person was liable to be forfeit as a 'deodand' (gift to God). You will normally see the value of a deodand (for example a horse or the branch of a tree) recorded in inquest records. In reality the item went not to God, but to the crown, or in rare cases to the deceased's family. The crown also confiscated the property (or took an equivalent fine) of anyone convicted of murder or who had committed suicide, and a value for such property will also be recorded. This example from 1552 is taken from *Sussex Coroners' Inquests 1458–1558* by R. Hunnisett (Sussex Record Society 1985).

> Margaret late the wife of Richard Yeman of Nutley went into Egellsewoode in Ashdown Forest in Nutley and by mischance frighted a man felling a beche [beech tree] worth 16d; the tree fell and one of its branches by misadventure struck her head, scattering her brains and killing her.

Although many coroners had legal or medical qualifications, these were not obligatory until 1926. The only criterion needed for the post was to be a landholder, while in medieval times most coroners were chosen from the upper echelons of society. The post was first salaried in 1860; although from 1752 coroners were paid £1 for each inquest conducted and could claim travelling expenses too. Before this they were entitled to receive a fee of thirteen shillings and four pence for every inquest that led to a verdict of murder. Many, but not all, coroners held office for life and the post could remain in one family for several generations.

Up to 1888 a coroner's jurisdiction was county-wide, but there were usually several coroners in a county and they allocated themselves informal jurisdictional boundaries within it. Many boroughs and other jurisdictions such as the Cinque Ports in Kent and Sussex, the City of London and the Dean and Chapter of Westminster had the right to appoint a coroner for their own area. In 1888 new coroners' districts were created with one coroner responsible for each. From then on they were elected by the newly-formed county councils rather than local freeholders.

Up to 1926 an inquest took place before a coroner and a jury of between thirteen and twenty-three men. The jury would assess the evidence before them and, under the guidance of the coroner, reach a verdict as to the cause of death. Both the coroner and the jury had to view the body in order for the inquest to be legal. They would note any relevant wounds or marks but, despite this, inquests were notably lacking in any forensic evidence before the late 1860s. Funds were first provided to pay for medical witnesses to attend inquests, and for post-mortems to be carried out to determine the cause of death, in 1836. This was a result of a growing concern that murders were being committed using poison and were going undetected. Before this date, although post-mortems were regularly carried out in the name of medical research, they were rarely part of an inquest and there were many verdicts of 'sudden death through natural causes' that did not indicate the actual cause of death. The Births and Deaths Registration Act of 1836 made the production of a death certificate necessary before burial could legally take place. If burial did take place without it, the clergyman responsible had seven days in which he could notify the registrar before he was liable to prosecution. This law was affirmed and extended by the Births and Deaths Registration Act of 1874, which emphasized that, in the case of the involvement of a coroner, the death certificate could not be issued or the body buried until authorization to do so had been received from the coroner, although in some rare cases burial still did go ahead with no certificate!

After the Coroners' Amendment Act of 1926 juries were reduced in number to between seven and eleven people, but they could only reach a lawful verdict if a minimum of all but two members were in agreement. For most cases after 1926 the coroner also had the power to sit alone without a jury if he thought it appropriate.

During the First World War inquests into air-raid victims were carried out in much the usual manner, despite pressure from the government to cut back on such investigations. During the Second World War inquests were not routinely held into deaths that clearly resulted from war activities, although from 14 March 1941 an inquest was carried out if a body could not be identified, or was not recovered.

A coroner and his jury had no power to convict suspected criminals for causing someone's death. Their role was, and still is, simply to establish the facts of what happened. If it appeared that someone might be to blame, the coroner had the power to pass him on to the criminal court system to stand trial. By contrast, today he will halt the inquest at the first indication of criminal involvement and pass the case on to the Crown Prosecution Service. Therefore, although most inquests deal with accidental or natural deaths, you may occasionally find that an inquest report leads you to further research in criminal records.

The Records and Where to Find Them

For many years inquest records were regarded as the personal property of the coroner. There was no requirement to preserve them until 1921. From this date any records dated before 1875 had to be preserved, although, sadly, many had already been destroyed. Rather bizarrely, later documents were not granted similar protection and once they are fifteen years old may legally be destroyed by the coroner. Many have, however, been deposited in local record offices. For privacy reasons inquest files are closed to the public until they are seventy-five years old, although registers of deaths and other administrative papers are accessible once they are thirty years old.

From the mid-nineteenth century the easiest method of locating details of your ancestor's inquest is usually the local newspaper; the majority will have been reported at some length. See Chapter 5 for details of how to access them. Many local newspapers carried a section specifically for inquest reports, while in others you will find them either in a roundup of district news or on the same page as obituaries. When you are searching, remember that inquests were usually held within a few days of the death, although the actual inquest might run on for several weeks. If there is no newspaper report, or if the case you are looking for pre-dates the earliest local paper, you will have to turn to original inquest records.

The easiest way to determine which records have survived is to use *Coroners' Records in England and Wales* by Jeremy Gibson and Colin Rogers (3rd edn, The Family History Partnership, 2009), which not only gives a useful introduction to the subject, but also a full geographical listing of surviving coroners' records and their location. It also has a good glossary and bibliography and provides a list of coroners' districts between 1888 and 1902. The inquest will have taken place in the district in which the person died.

Although some people may find it upsetting to read a detailed inquest report of an ancestor's tragic demise, it will provide a wealth of detail about his life. In a case where suicide was a possibility, great attention will be given to the deceased's personality and his state of mind in the days leading up to his death, in order to determine whether or not he took his own life. This was important for several reasons. Suicide was a criminal offence up to 1961 (although not in Scotland), while up to 1870 his goods could be confiscated by the crown, although this was rarely enforced after the early eighteenth century. There were also issues surrounding the burial of suicides in consecrated ground. It was not until the burial amendment acts of the nineteenth century that attitudes concerning the burial of

County of London.

CORONER'S OFFICER'S REPORT CONCERNING DEATH.

Full name, age, occupation, and address of deceased. If a married woman, widow, or child, state husband's or father's full name, address, and occupation. If an illegitimate child, mother's full name, occupation, and address.	*Joseph Edwin Archer 31 Years Commercial Traveller 147 Blyth Wood Rd Ilford*
State *where* and *when* (day and hour) the deceased died, or was found dying or dead.	*S.E. & C. D. Railway London Bridge 3.50 P.M Wed. 28 August*
Full Name and address of any legally qualified Medical Practitioner who has seen the deceased either before or after death; say which. If before death, state duration of attendance, and whether medical certificate of the cause of death is with-held or refused.	*Mr Camps Guy's Hospital*
If any known illness or injury existed before death, state, if possible, the nature of it, and its duration.	*Revolver shot through head*
If negligence or blame is imputed— say *to* whom; and *by* whom alleged.	*none*
If life insured, state Office or Society, how long, and what amount.	*Septре Life Insurance*
State the supposed cause of death, if known or suspected, and the circumstances relating to it, and all further particulars. (The Constable should state whether it was a sudden death, or whether it was a violent death, as by poisoning, wounds, burns or scalds, accident, suicide, neglect, ill-usage, or if involved in mystery, &c., and give particulars.) (When anything poisonous is known or is suspected to have caused the death, the remaining portion should be put under seal by the constable, who shall dispose of it as the Coroner shall direct. In difficult or doubtful cases the Constable should attend at the Coroner's office for instructions.)	*The deceased who was found in one of the lavatorys on the platform of London Bridge Station has been suffering from a disease of the brain but it was not thought he would*

attempt his life. He was found at 3.50 P.M by Walter Heathfield and bleeding from a wound in the head and with the assistance of Percy Chambers + P.C. 13 M. R. he was conveyed to Guys Hospital where Mr Camps pronounced him dead

(This page and opposite) *Front page of the coroner's report into the death of Joseph Archer and an extract from the post-mortem report, both dated 1901. The post-mortem report showed that Joseph had 'a bullet wound to palate between the 2nd and 3rd molars on the right side traversing the base of the skull . . .' and concluded that he 'shot himself through the mouth'. (City of London, London Metropolitan Archives. CLA/042/1Q/02/02/001)* suicides in churchyards were generally relaxed. Even so, it was not until 1882 that a churchyard burial with some form of religious service was allowed. Prior to 1823 suicides were usually buried outside the churchyard, often at a crossroads. This was possibly because of the superstitious belief that burial at a crossroads disorientated the suicide's tormented soul, which would otherwise try to find its way back home! In more modern times most life assurance companies would not pay out if the insured had taken his own life. If there was no doubt that someone had taken his own life, a jury would often bring a verdict of 'suicide while temporarily insane'. This was not just to spare the family's feelings; some life assurance companies could be persuaded to pay out given such a verdict, while burial might also be allowed in consecrated ground and fines might be waived by the government.

The types of record you may find in connection with an inquest vary, but the main one is the 'inquest' or 'coroner's report' (sometimes called an 'inquisition'). This will list the name of the coroner, the jury members and the deceased, provide a summary of the findings of the jury and record the verdict. Then there are 'depositions': these are verbatim witness statements taken during the course of the inquest from next of kin or those people who last saw the deceased before his death. Witnesses usually include the person who found the body and, frequently, a police officer who was called to the scene. It is these records that often prove to be most useful for the family historian, revealing details of the deceased's daily life. They can provide information about his personality, his family and his relations with them, his work, his health and any other events that may be relevant to his demise. A report in the *Westmorland Gazette* in the 1880s, concerning the accidental death of a labourer called Stephen Simpson, revealed that Stephen and his wife Jane had been separated for over two years when his death occurred; information unlikely to be found elsewhere. Depositions can also provide an insight into what life was like at that time for someone of the deceased's class. In the case of an accident, full details will be provided by any eye-witnesses and, from the nineteenth century, you may also find statements from doctors who attended the deceased or viewed his body after death, as well as notes from any post-mortem examination. By their nature the latter are explicit, so if you are squeamish – be warned!

Other documents may include separate lists of jury members and documentation ordering the calling of a jury for the case. Where a body is initially unidentified there may be later documents signed by a next of kin formally identifying the deceased.

From the late nineteenth century onwards an increasing number of inquest records were completed on pre-printed forms with gaps for individual case details to be entered. Even so, any notes, especially those taken during the inquest itself, may still be difficult to decipher. By this date you can expect to discover details of the deceased's address and occupation, doctors who attended him, previous illnesses, and any indication as to whether a third party was suspected to be in any way responsible for the death. You should also find details of the deceased's life assurance company where applicable. A good example is the report for Joseph Archer shown on page 86.

There may be other documents containing supporting evidence too. In 1894 Edward Coughlin, a railway shunter for the Great Northern Railway, was killed when he was crushed between two wagons in the goods depot at Farringdon, London. The inquest records consist of several pages of witness statements and also a diagram of the accident site.

You may also discover notices of deaths in institutions, which had to be

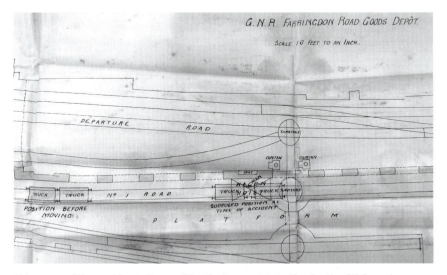

Diagram of the accident site used in the inquest into the death of Edward Coughlin, who was killed in a railway carriage shunting accident in 1894. (City of London, London Metropolitan Archives. CLA/041/IQ/03/76)

BETHLEM ROYAL HOSPITAL.

FORM No. 21.

(13)

NOTICE OF DEATH.

328   Date of Reception Order, the _28th_ day of _January_ 1900

hereby give you Notice, that _Charles Chase_

private Patient, received into this Hospital on the _2nd_ day of _February_ 1900

died therein on the _7th_ day of _September_ 1901

Signed _Theo. B. Hyslop_
Medical Officer of Bethlem Royal Hospital, London.

Dated the _9th_ day of _September_ 1901

STATEMENT RESPECTING THE ABOVE-NAMED PATIENT.

Name _Charles Chase_

Sex and Age _Male. 71 years_

Married, Single or Widowed _Married_

Profession or Occupation _Merchant_

Place of abode immediately before being placed under care and treatment (if known) ... _Church Place Pulborough, Sussex_

Apparent cause of death _Chronic Melancholia. Angina Pectoris_

Whether or not ascertained by post-mortem examination ... ... _Yes_

Time and any unusual circumstances attending the death; also a description of any injuries known to exist at time of death, or found subsequently on body of deceased _6.15 pm. 7th September 1901. Patient was apparently in robust physical health, walking in the garden. He suddenly complained of a pain in his heart & fell back into another patient's arms. The attendants immediately laid him on the ground & found life was extinct_

Duration of disease of which Patient died ... ... _Admitted into this Hospital. 2nd February 1900_

Names and description of persons present at the death ... ... _Frederick Howe & Alfred English. attendants_

Whether or not mechanical restraint was applied to deceased within seven days previously to death with its character and duration if so applied ... ... _No_

I hereby certify that the particulars contained in the above Statement are true.

The Coroner   **Signed** _Theo. B. Hyslop_
Medical Officer of Bethlem Royal Hospital.

The Notice of Death form for Charles Chase, who died in Bethlem Royal Hospital in 1901, provides details of his age, marital status and address as well as the circumstances and cause of his death. (City of London, London Metropolitan Archives CLRO/05/502/001 N7) completed whenever a death occurred in a prison, hospital or asylum, and were sent to the coroner. These often provide graphic detail of the inmate's health, medication and circumstances of death, as well as age, marital status and next of kin. If the death occurred in prison there will usually be details of the length of time spent in jail.

Where the coroner decided that an inquest was not necessary there may be surviving lists of 'no inquest cases' giving brief details of the deceased's name, date and cause of death. You may also find indexed registers of reported deaths that were made for the coroner's initial attention, or registers of inquests taken that name the deceased and verdict given, but give little further detail.

The majority of surviving coroners' records from 1752 onwards will be found in local record offices. From this date up to 1860 they were filed by the local Quarter Session courts, although you may find that some record offices have separated them out from the Quarter Session records. Many Quarter Session records have been summarized chronologically by record offices and now form part of their online catalogue or the Access to Archives (A2A) website. There are usually paper copies on the shelf at the record office too, which are easy to skim through. These summaries usually provide a fair bit of detail regarding the case, such as this typical example from Warwickshire:

> Mary Ann Jelfs aged 10 years accidentally killed by a threshing machine at Aston Cantlow. Depositions: John Smith of Grafton, labourer, John Ings of Henley-in-Arden surgeon, and Mary Jelfs, wife of John of Aston Cantlow, labourer, and mother of deceased.[1]

It is always worth ordering the original documents from the archive strong room, which will add further details. In this case the witness statements told how young Mary Ann was employed by John Lane, of Burton Farm at nearby Haselor, to put clover into the threshing machine. Her left arm was badly lacerated as a result of becoming entangled in the machine. She was pulled out of the machine and carried home to Aston Cantlow where the local surgeon amputated her arm; she died later.

It often pays to study inquest records that don't relate directly to your own family, but to other local inhabitants. You may well find that your family gets a mention. In this case the inquest took place at the Sun Inn, which belonged to my ancestor Charles Heritage. He was also a member of the jury, as were his brothers-in-law Stephen and Thomas Clements. There was also an expenses claim by the local constable, Anthony Edkins, amounting to £3 18s 10d with further expenses paid to three other constables from the neighbouring village of Haselor, all of whom were named. This all helps build up a picture of our ancestors' lives.

Because of the varying ways in which record office catalogues are compiled, it is worth using a variety of search terms when you make your online search. A search under 'coroners' records', 'inquest' or' inquisition' usually works well, but I have found that one of the best search terms to use is simply 'coroner'. They may also be filed under 'Quarter Sessions'. Be wary if you use 'inquisition' as a search term as it is also used to denote a type of manorial document called the 'inquisition post mortem', and this is nothing to do with inquest reports! Jeremy Gibson's guide *Quarter Sessions Records for Family Historians* (5th edn, The Family History Partnership, 2007) is also a useful finding aid for these records.

If there are no surviving records before 1860 you may be able to locate coroners' bills. These were also filed with the Quarter Sessions records and list expenses incurred for each case. They will normally give the deceased's name, place and date of inquest and the verdict.

Before 1752 coroners' records were filed with the various royal criminal courts (the Eyre and the King's Bench up to about 1420 and the Assize Judges from 1487 up to 1752.) It is uncertain where they were filed between 1420 and 1487. These records will be found at TNA. Although coroners were supposed to send in their inquests to the various courts on a regular basis, bear in mind that not every coroner complied! TNA's website has several helpful research guides on coroners' inquests and assize records which I recommend you read if you wish to track down records before 1752.

The easiest way to access coroners' records before 1752, bearing in mind that pre-1733 records will be in Latin, is to search for published transcripts

---

A Selection of Published Inquest Records

R.F. Hunnisett *Calendar of Nottinghamshire Coroners' Inquests 1485-1557* (Thoroton Society, vol XXV, 1969)

R.F. Hunnisett Sussex Coroners' Inquests 1458-1558 (Sussex Record Society, vol LXXIV, 1985)

R.F. Hunnisett Sussex Coroners' Inquests 1558-1603 (Public Record Office, 1996)

R.F. Hunnisett Sussex Coroners' Inquests 1603-1688 (Public Record Office, 1998)

R.F. Hunnisett Wiltshire Coroners' Bills 1752-1796. (Wiltshire Record Society, Vol. 36)

R.R. Sharpe Calendar of Letter Books of the City of London (1900) has a copy of the coroner's rolls 1276-8 (available at London Metropolitan Archives)

Select Cases from the Coroners Rolls 1265-1413 (Seldon Society, Vol IX, 1896)

or summaries. Roy Hunnisett, a specialist in coroners' records, published many books containing translations and summaries of records for various areas, notably for Sussex and Wiltshire. It is always worth searching the internet to see what is available, either as an online book, or what has been published on the subject by various record societies such as the British Record Society.

Determining whether there was an Inquest

After the introduction of death certificates in 1837 it becomes easier to determine whether or not there was an inquest into your ancestor's death. From 1875 details of the inquest will be recorded on the certificate in column seven and the cause of death will be the verdict given by the jury. As mentioned earlier, in some cases the coroner would decide that an inquest was not required. He might typically make this decision after a post-mortem had clearly identified the cause of death and where there were no suspicious circumstances. In this case the fact that a post-mortem took place but no inquest was held will be noted on the certificate, usually with the phrase 'Certificate issued after Post-Mortem. No inquest on authority of so and so coroner.' Before 1875, although details of the inquest are not given, the informant will still be the coroner, while the cause of death is often a giveaway!

During your research you may spot other clues that lead you to an inquest report. In one branch of my family I noticed the burials of several family members within six months of each other. This prompted me to look in the newspaper in case there was further information. Here I found an inquest report for one of them. He had drowned, possibly through taking his own life, following the deaths of the three other family members.

Both burial entries and gravestones may indicate a cause of death, especially where it was violent or tragic. For example, the gravestone of Eleanor Roberts in Hyde Park Cemetery, Doncaster, states she was 'killed in an explosion in Baxter Gate Doncaster' in 1880. This clearly suggests there is going to be further information available, either as surviving inquest records or in the newspaper. In this case there was a lengthy inquest into the explosion, which took place one night in the shop of local gunsmith George Hanson, and killed three people. Twenty-eight people were called as witnesses and the inquest was adjourned several times because the exact cause of the explosion and ensuing fire could not be determined. The incident was initially reported as a news item in the papers (not just locally, but across the country) followed by regular accounts of the inquest, which turned out to be rather protracted and involved a full investigation of the scene of the fire. It also provided a wealth of detail about Mr Hanson and his wife, who were also killed in the incident. Eleanor Roberts lived next door, where she ran a hosiery business together with her sisters Ann and

The grave of Eleanor Roberts at Hyde Park Cemetery, Doncaster, recorded her tragic death in an explosion of gunpowder. (Image courtesy of the World Burial Index, www.burialindex.com)

Mary. They slept in a separate bedroom to Eleanor and were rescued by firemen: Eleanor's body was recovered from the kitchen. Her bedroom was above and the roof and floor of her bedroom were taken out by the explosion. The post-mortem stated that she had died from suffocation, which was evident from 'a fine frothy mucous below the larynx'. Her body was also extremely badly burned. Mr and Mrs Hanson died of crush injuries.

With the growing number of record office catalogues now online and the increasing digitization of newspapers, finding references to inquests even before 1837 is going to become much easier.

Springboards to Other Records

Inquest records not only provide a wonderful insight into your ancestors' lives, but can often lead you to other sources where you learn more about your family. In the case study of Edwin Barnes (see pages 96–101) I was able to find out more about where he worked from trade directories and maps, while learning about his premature death meant I could explore the consequences this had for the rest of the family.

In cases where the records mention a life assurance policy you can check to see if the records of the relevant company survive. Survival rates are not great, but well worth looking for from the late nineteenth century, by which time life assurance had become affordable for the majority of families. Some companies offered it as a perk for their staff as well. Surviving assurance records usually consist of either registers of insured people with details of their address, age, and how much they were insured for or, occasionally, the actual proposal forms. These potentially include a

Life Assurance documents provide details of the insured and other family members. (Author's collection).

physical description of the person, details of his health and the health of other family members. They will be found at local record offices or may remain with the assurance company or its successor, while copies of the policy documents may be found among family papers. In the case of the explosion at Baxter Gate the inquest mentions that Mr Hanson had a fire insurance policy with the Manchester Fire Insurance Company and it would be worthwhile to see if any policy records for the company survive for this date. You can do this by checking the online catalogue for the local record office, but also check the A2A catalogue. It's a good idea not to limit the search to a particular record office or area, as many insurance companies were later bought out by other companies and the records could end up in a record office far distant from the place where the company originally had its headquarters.

If an inquest jury decided that a third party was responsible for the manslaughter or murder of your ancestor this may lead you to criminal records that give further details of the case. Bear in mind that in such cases both coroners' inquest records and criminal records provide details not only about the deceased, but also the person allegedly responsible for their death, so you can use them to learn about both the victim and accused. Locating the criminal records you want is often not straightforward because, apart from a short period in the nineteenth century, the records were not centralized. As mentioned already, early inquest records will be filed with the records of the King's Bench or Assize courts up to 1752, but there are many different types of records involved in a criminal trial and they were usually filed separately according to record type rather than by individual case. Therefore, you will usually have to make several searches for each case. The records will either be held at the local record office, prison or at TNA. There is insufficient room here to go into depth about criminal records, but here are a few pointers.

Some databases are now available online, including the Old Bailey Proceedings from 1674 to 1913, which gives extensive details of criminal trials for Middlesex and the City of London and can be found at www.oldbaileyonline.org. You can search the database by name or keyword.

If you wish to find out whether someone sent for trial as a result of a coroner's inquest was found guilty or not, and the date falls between 1791 and 1892, then the Criminal Registers held at TNA (HO 26 and 27) are on Ancestry and list those charged with criminal offences, verdicts, sentences and dates of execution where applicable. Irish Prison Registers 1790–1924 are online at Findmypast Ireland (findmypast.ie).

Gaol delivery books and prison registers are also useful for finding the verdict of a trial and may be found either at TNA or at local archives; more likely the latter after 1878. TNA has several essential research guides on how to locate both criminal and assize records, while David Hawking's

Criminal Ancestors (The History Press, 2009) is the definitive guide. Some assize records have been published. An easy way to see what is available is to search the online catalogues of major online booksellers using the key words 'assize records'.

Ireland

The National Archives of Ireland holds coroner's records dating from the nineteenth and twentieth centuries (although many were lost in the fire at the record office in 1922). The Public Record Office of Northern Ireland also holds records from 1872 onwards, but again not all records survive. It has indexed the majority of its inquest papers for the period 1872–1920 and these are searchable at www.proni.gov.uk as part of the 'Name Search' index. Original documents for this period are open to the public.

Scotland

In Scotland investigation into sudden or suspicious deaths is the responsibility of the procurator fiscal where the person died and there is no equivalent of the English inquest. If a death was suspicious an initial cause of death would be recorded when the death was registered. Once the procurator fiscal had investigated, this would either be confirmed or corrected, according to his findings, and an entry made to that effect in the Register for Corrected Entries (See Chapter 1). These corrections could be made many months after the death.

There were also Fatal Accident Inquiries (FAI), which were introduced in 1895 and conducted by the procurator fiscal in front of a sheriff. They investigated deaths that had occurred through industrial accidents or in prisons, although an FAI might be held in other cases if it was considered to be in the public interest. You will find these either at National Records Scotland or at the local sheriff's court. For further information see www.nas.gov.uk/guides/FAI.asp

---

Case Study: The Inquest into the Death of Edwin Barnes

Although my ancestor Edwin Barnes was born in 1845 in Staplehurst, Kent, his family moved to London when he was a teenager. Here he married Sarah Ayley in 1865 and went on to have three children; Edwin and Frederick (both born in Lambeth) and Mary Ann, who was born in Newport, South Wales, in 1875, where Edwin presumably temporarily located the family for work reasons. By the 1881 census they were once again in south London and at this point, keen to trace the line further back in time, I left my research into Edwin and Sarah, making the presumption that there was not much more to discover. Several years later, however, I stumbled across Mary Ann, aged

---

Three Crowns Square, where Edwin Barnes met with his fatal accident, was on the site of what is today Borough Market. It is shown here in 2007. (Author's collection)

fifteen, in a 'Home for Fatherless Girls' in Brixton. Clearly my presumption that there was nothing more to learn about Sarah and Edwin was incorrect! I soon found Edwin's entry in the death index and hastily ordered the certificate. It was the start of a fascinating trail of information that opened my eyes to the circumstances facing the Barnes family after Edwin's death, but which has also left many questions unanswered.

The death certificate gave the cause of death as 'inflammation of the lungs caused by a blow on the eye by a box'. I knew that Edwin worked as a wine cellarman, so this surely had to be connected? What I could not understand was how a blow to his eye would result in inflammation of the lungs. I was unable to locate a report of the inquest in the local newspapers, but the inquest records survived. This consisted of the main inquest form listing the coroner, jury members, brief details of the verdict and a set of full notes, obviously hurriedly written during the inquest and extremely hard to read. Once deciphered, however, they gave full details of Edwin's demise.

The accident occurred about a week before Christmas 1882. The first witness was Sarah Barnes, who stated the following:

The Home for Fatherless Girls in Brixton where Mary Ann Barnes lived after Edwin's death. Today it has been converted to flats. (Author's collection)

I am Sarah Ann Barnes of 1 Susanna Place, Horselydown. Edwin was my husband. He was 37 and a wine cellarman. On the morning of the accident he was in good health but when he came home for lunch his eye was bandaged up. I asked him what had happened and he replied that he had had a case fall on his head. A man was upstairs letting down a case and it slipped and fell on his head. He said it was an accident. He went back to work but during the week he fell ill. Mr Gittins saw him. He did nothing about the eye but said he had bronchitis. He saw him for a week but he got worse. The blackness went off from the eye but still he got worse and I called in Dr Boney. It was his chest and breathing that was bad. He died on Wednesday afternoon. He had no other hurt. He continued to work to the Saturday night before Christmas.

Mary Ann Barnes in later life. (Photo courtesy of Jan Feist)

The next witness to be called was Frederick William Debnam, who identified himself as the cellar foreman at Messrs Mart and Company, Three Crowns Square, Southwark. He explained that he was lowering an empty wine case by hand. It was not heavy but it was long and awkward and as he was turning it the deceased came along and he was unable to avoid hitting him.

I swear I tried to avoid him but the corner of the case struck him just by the eye. It did not appear to stun him. It was more of a cut than a blow. The case fell to the ground. It was a case I could easily manage.

He goes on to say that Edwin bathed his eye and put 'sticking plaster' on it.

Another colleague, called William Chapman, was also in the cellar at the time. He said that the case was being lowered in 'a strange manner' and hit Edwin on the eye. Edwin fell to the ground and William asked him if he was all right. In contrast to the previous witness, William stated that Edwin was stunned and could not answer: his head was bleeding next to the eye. William also said that Edwin's health was usually very good.

The rest of the notes consist of a statement made by Mr Gittins, the local doctor, who had initially attended Edwin and also Dr Boney, who was called in by Sarah a few days later. Dr Boney said that by the time he was called to attend, Edwin was 'groaning and half delirious and showing signs of congestion of the brain.' Edwin had a fever with a temperature of 106 degrees and was bringing up 'matter' as a result of inflammation of the lungs. It was his opinion that his death was caused by inflammation of the lungs resulting from internal bleeding as a result of the blow to the head.

The jury brought a verdict of 'accidental death.'

Apart from giving me full details of how Edwin died, the inquest gave me an insight into the sort of work he did and the potential hazards involved. It also showed me the great contrast between attitudes to work in that day and my own. Imagine being involved in such an accident and then going back to work after lunch these days!

I also discovered several important new facts, including details of Edwin's employer (Messrs Mart and Co.) and his work address (Three Crowns Square). A trade directory for this time confirmed that 'S. Mart and Co. Wine and Spirit Merchants' traded from there and showed that they were wine and spirit merchants rather than importers. They also had premises at Southwark Chambers. Further investigation using old maps showed me that Three Crowns Square was on the site of Borough Market in Southwark, so I was able to visit the site of Edwin's fatal accident. From Sarah Barnes's statement I also learned exactly where the family lived in 1883; a twenty-minute walk from Edwin's place of work. I was able to use this information, together with that from census returns and certificates, to compile a list of addresses where they had lived during their married life. Edwin and Sarah were relatively poor and I wondered if the 'Mr Gittins', to whom Sarah referred, was not actually a qualified doctor and whether she had only paid for a proper doctor when Edwin failed to recover. I was able to check this on the Medical Register for 1883, which is available on Ancestry, and this showed that John Gittins was indeed a qualified doctor practising in the Horselydown area.

The inquest record prompted me to try and track down the remaining family in census and other records in the years after Edwin's death to see how they coped in its aftermath. To this day I have been unable to find out what happened to Sarah Barnes: there is no definite trace of her death or remarriage. By the time of the next census in 1891 Mary Ann is in the 'Home for Fatherless Girls', while the two boys are in their twenties and appear as lodgers with two separate families. Edwin junior followed in his father's footsteps and became a wine cellarman, although, sadly, he died aged twenty-eight of tuberculosis. My great-grandfather Frederick appears to have lost all touch with Mary Ann and never mentioned the fact that he had a younger sister to anyone within living memory. It was only in the twentieth century that the two branches of the family were reunited when Mary Ann's great-granddaughter Janette traced me via the internet. The after-effects of Edwin's premature death appear to have greatly affected Mary Ann, making her a rather sad person who never mentioned her childhood. Further research showed that the 'Home for Fatherless Girls' was in Barrington Road, Brixton. This was a charitable institution funded by the Church of England, which aimed to train orphaned girls for domestic service. It housed some 300 girls at that time and the building remains today, having been converted to flats.

Chapter 5

NEWSPAPERS AND MAGAZINES AS A SOURCE FOR DEATH RECORDS

Newspapers are an excellent source for both obituaries and inquest reports, which are in turn two of the most fruitful sources for finding out more about an ancestor's life. Contrary to popular belief obituaries were not just the remit of the better off sections of society, and whether they are of great length or simply a short paragraph they provide useful information for the genealogist. They are especially helpful before the advent of death certificates in 1837, when they may provide information regarding the circumstances of a death. They may also reveal facts about your ancestor's life that are unlikely to be found elsewhere and give you an insight into his personality; the latter has to come with the rejoinder that obituaries naturally tend to concentrate on our ancestors' good points rather than their bad!

Although the most usual place to find obituaries is in local newspapers, if your ancestor was a member of a religious group, trade, or craft that produced its own journal you may find an obituary there. For example, my relative Richard Wilson, an evangelist with the Plymouth Brethren, has a long obituary together with a photograph in *The Believers' Pathway*, a magazine for bible students and Christian workers. I recently bought a second-hand copy of the trade magazine *The Draper's Record* dated 1937 and this carried a column of obituaries for people in the trade. Even a local parish or school magazine may carry obituaries, as will public school magazines, so keep an open mind about where to look.

We looked in detail at coroners' records in Chapter 4 and details of most inquests were reported in local newspapers from the mid-nineteenth century, often making it the easiest way to obtain information about your ancestor's demise.

Photograph from the obituary for Richard Wilson in the publication Believer's Pathway, *1929. (Author's collection)*

The Background to Using Newspapers as Sources for Death Records

Until recently family historians tended to neglect local newspapers, mainly because access was limited to regional libraries and archives, the British Newspaper Library in London, or the respective National Libraries of Wales, Scotland and Ireland. Although many newspapers had been copied onto microfilm, few had been indexed, which often meant a lengthy search through more than one newspaper with no guarantee of finding anything of interest. Searching newspapers on microfilm is not only time-consuming, but it is also incredibly easy to overlook the small paragraph that relates to the event you are looking for.

Things are changing rapidly in this respect with a growing number of newspapers being digitized and made available online. Although the number of newspapers currently available in this way is still only relatively small (e.g. the British Library has digitized about one per cent of its whole collection) the growing use of Optical Character Recognition (OCR) to convert scanned newspaper images to text means the researcher can use a search engine to hunt for any key word or phrase within the entire contents of digitized collections. This not only saves much time, but reduces the risk of overlooking the required information. It also makes speculative searches of newspapers far more appealing.

Today we make a distinction between 'national' and 'local' papers, but up to the late nineteenth century the distinction was actually one of newspapers published in London or newspapers published in the provinces. Either can be of use to you in your search for death records, although it is usually the newspapers produced in the locality where your ancestor lived or died that hold most potential. The earliest provincial papers, such as the *Stamford Mercury*, the *Norwich Post* and *Berrow's Worcester Journal* (initially known as the *Worcester Post Man*) were all established by the first quarter of the eighteenth century and nearly all major provincial towns were publishing a paper by the 1820s. Although provincial newspapers of this time carried local adverts, there was precious little local news in them and they usually simply replicated news printed in the London papers. Many printers ran a newspaper as a sideline to their main printing business and would subscribe to a London paper from which they would cut and paste news into their own publication. There were no news reporters and the decision as to what went into the newspaper lay solely with the printer. These papers only began to flourish as purveyors of local news after 1855 when the government abolished stamp duty on newspapers followed by duty on paper in 1861. A third duty on advertising had already been abolished in 1853 and the abolition of these led to a flurry of new local newspapers around the country. Many were short-lived, lasting only a few months or a few years, but some are still with us today. Fewer taxes and the introduction of cheaper printing meant that newspapers became affordable for the majority of the public, while the increasing education of the lower classes encouraged an interest in local politics and debate. This in turn increased the demand for local news.

At the same time Britain's rapidly expanding transport network meant that London papers could be delivered to the provinces much more easily. There was, therefore, little point in provincial papers reproducing world news anymore, and they began to concentrate on local news, with many towns boasting not one but several local papers. The result of this for the researcher looking for death records is that from the mid-nineteenth century you can expect a far greater number of obituaries and inquest reports to appear.

National Daily Newspapers

Newspapers were first published in London in the 1620s but the first daily was the *Daily Courant*, founded in 1702. *The Morning Post* and *The Times* (originally *The Daily Universal Register*) were first published in the late eighteenth century and both carried obituaries. *The London Gazette* (established 1665) and its sister papers the *Edinburgh* and *Belfast Gazette* were the official voice of the government and the place where public notices (such as bankruptcies) were required to be placed by law. As such the *Gazette* carried far fewer obituaries than many other newspapers. They are, however, all freely available and searchable online and will often produce pleasing results if a death has been under scrutiny in the public eye in any way. The following is an example from the *London Gazette* dated 27 August 1832:

> HERE AS it hath been humbly represented unto the King, that Mrs. Jane Whitham, Marine Store-Dealer, residing at No. 30, Princess Street, Lambeth, in the county of Surrey, was barbarously murdered in her house, between the hours of four and seven o'clock in the evening of Thursday the 19th day of August instant, by some evil disposed person or persons unknown.
>
> His Majesty, for the better apprehending and bringing to justice the persons concerned in the murder before mentioned, is hereby pleased to promise His most gracious pardon to any one of them (except the person who actually committed the said murder) who shall discover his accomplice or accomplices therein, so that he, she, or they may be apprehended and convicted thereof.
>
> ROBERT PEEL

Similarly the death of a lowly ancestor may feature in a paper such as *The Times* as a news article or perhaps a letter to the editor. A random search of *The Times* Digital Archive for any of my Heritage ancestors revealed a lengthy account of the sad fate of William Heritage in 1831. A teenage sailor, he suffered severe bullying in the form of excessive use of the cat-o'-nine-tails at the hands of the ship's boatswain. In order to avoid any further subjection to the cat William eventually threw himself overboard to his death and, as a result, the ship's captain was court martialled. William's father, in a letter to the editor of *The Times*, wrote about his concern that some evidence had not been brought out in court and his letter includes full details of the case. Without digitization, items such as this would frequently lie undiscovered by the researcher.

105

News items concerning wills and probate matters may also occasionally be found in the national papers if they were newsworthy. Most relate to larger estates, such as the report in *The Times* of 5 October 1801 concerning the will of Mr Robertson of Stockwell, which was challenged by his family and set aside by the Court of Chancery on the grounds that it was not drawn up correctly. Mr Robertson had intended the proceeds of his estate to provide funds for the establishment of a Botanic Garden, but after the court's decision all funds were divided between his family! Various reports in *The Times* during 1785 included the indictment of someone for assuming a false identity in an attempt to gain probate of a will and, by contrast, the official granting by the king of the coat of arms and surname of 'Charlton' to Nicholas Lechmere, according to the will of his late uncle, Sir Francis Charlton.

Obituaries

There is a common misconception that it was only our richer ancestors who merited an obituary in the newspaper, but as we shall see this is not true and you should routinely search for an obituary for each of your ancestors no matter how poor you feel he was or how insignificant you feel his life would have been.

Although the heyday of the local newspapers can be seen to date from the late 1850s up to, arguably, the late twentieth century, you will still find obituaries in provincial newspapers before the 1850s. Most newspapers would have had a small 'Births, Marriages and Deaths' section and here the printer would insert details of any deaths that he thought were of interest. These might range from someone who was well-known locally to a death that was of interest for other reasons, perhaps because of the deceased's tender years or the circumstances of death. Some would have consisted of merely one line, others of several lines. Be warned that the 'Births, Marriages and Deaths' sections are often tucked away in a corner and very easy to miss!

When my ancestor Edward Dickinson died in 1821 I found just a one-line obituary for him in the *Westmorland Gazette*. It pays to check more than one newspaper where possible, however, and I found this much more detailed account in the *Kendal and Westmorland Advertiser*:

> At his house, at Garnet Bridge, in this county, on Sunday last, aged 39, after a long and painful illness, which he bore with christian patience and fortitude, Mr Edward Dickinson, miller and maltster. He has left a wife and eight children to lament his loss – he was a kind husband and a most affectionate parent – a man of the strictest integrity in respect to his worldly dealings – and was universally respected amongst a numerous acquaintance.

Although it is frustrating not to know the exact cause of Edward's death, the obituary at least gives us some indication of its nature, which is particularly useful as there were, of course, no death certificates at this time. In some cases the cause of death will be given, but bear in mind that newspapers are not always accurate in what they report! In this case we learn that Edward left eight children, but I can only locate the baptisms of seven and I need to consider the fact that the printer may have made a mistake when he created this entry. Whether his information was based on personal knowledge, from direct conversation with the family or perhaps from a less reliable source we shall never know, and I may never be able to fully assess the accuracy of this piece of information.

In the same edition of the newspaper is the following entry:

At Wood Head Catterlen, near Penrith, Margaret Turnbull, aged 19, sister to the youth whose death we mentioned a fortnight ago.

The printer obviously felt that this was sufficiently newsworthy to merit an entry because of the connection with the previous death. Glancing back two weeks we find the following:

Lately, Mister William Turnbull of Wood Head Catterlen, aged 11. A youth whose superior qualifications, united to an amiable disposition endeared him to his numerous friends.

No date is given, merely the term 'Lately', which goes to prove that, especially at this early date in the development of the local newspaper, you should be prepared to extend your search for obituaries for several weeks after someone's death. We have seen in previous chapters how it is important to research the deaths of your ancestors' siblings and especially any who died at a young age. Newspapers are another excellent source for such research. In this case, learning about the sad losses the Turnbull family experienced is an important part of understanding their lives. Imagine the trauma caused by losing first their eleven-year-old son and a few weeks later their nineteen-year-old daughter.

A particularly good source for early obituaries is *The Gentleman's Magazine*. Founded in 1731, it published news on a wide range of topics intended to interest the educated person. Its obituaries tend towards those that are generally newsworthy, such as these three examples from September 1744:

Aug. 31 Capt. John Scott, formerly in the Bristol Trade, taken ill in the Meeting-House, at Horsleydown, and died in a few Minutes. His Brother dropt down dead in the Ground, at his Funeral.

Gazette.   30 November 1955

LATE MR. JAMES DICKINSON, GRANGE

The funeral of Mr. James Dickinson, Heightside, Grange, took place at the Cartmel burial ground last Thursday, and was preceded by a service at St. Paul's Church, Grange, at which the Rev. B. D. Lloyd Wilson, vicar, officiated. Mr. A. Pixton was at the organ and the large congregation included many Cartmel residents. The Rev. E. A. Mould conducted the committal service at the village burial ground.

The chief mourners were Mr. and Mrs. Kenneth Spoor (son-in-law and daughter), Mr. L. E. H. Perry (son-in-law), Misses E. and B. Dickinson (sisters), Mrs. George Dickinson, Mrs. E. Dickinson and Mrs. J. Dickinson (sisters-in-law), Mr. L. Breech (brother-in-law), Mr. W. Dickinson, Kendal (cousin), Mr. George Dickinson, Mr. Peter Dickinson, Mr. Tony Dickinson, Mr Michael Dickinson, Mr. Bernard Dickinson, Mr. Cleasby, Mr. and Mrs. W. Dickinson, Ulverston and Mr. J. J. Dickinson (nephews and nieces).

Ulverston Rural Council was represented by Mr. J. H. Park (chairman), who was accompanied by Mrs. Park,

Coun. W. R. Owen and Coun. R. Moore (Allithwaite), the Cartmel Steeplechase Co. by Capt. H. D. Pain, Mr. J. Newby Parker, Mr. G. D. Muncaster and Mr. A. Lewis (secretary), Grange Golf Club by Mr. S. Broadbent, Mr. P. A. Birley, Mr. S. Snowden, Mr. J. F. Broadbent, Mr. W. Birkett, Mr. F. Taylor, Mr. W. E. Quirk, Mr. J. C. Haydock, Mr. H. Walker and Mr. L. Hill, and old employees of Cark Corn Mills by Mr. J. Burrow, Mr. Crowe, Mr. J. Parrington and Mr. Walker. Others present included Mr. H. Eden Smith, Dr. R. L. Rhodes, Dr. Cox, Mr. R. B. Jackson, Mr. W. R. Cape, Mr. F. Wike Mr. E. W. Jackson, Mr. J. Higginbottom, Mr. J. M. Hutton, Mr. J. Asplin, Mrs. J. J. Spoor. Mrs. Michaelson, Mrs. H. B. Ferry and Miss P. Molyneux, Mr. G. Lawrence (Holker), Mrs. E. Brunskill (Crosthwaite), Miss J. Perry, Miss Cleasby, Mrs. M. Whitwell, Mr. R. Wright (Holker), Mr. H. Teasdale, Mr. J Hulme, Mr. J. Rawsthorn, Mr. J. Sargent, Mrs. Campbell, Mr. H. Wilson, Mr. F. Crowe, Mr. J. B. Hollywell, Mr. J. Hayton, Miss K. Allanby, Miss M. J. Allanby and Miss L. Allanby, Miss Dean and Miss E. Dean, Mrs. T. Dixon, Miss Rawlinson and Mr. G. Cannon.

Among the floral tributes were wreaths from Grange Golf Club and Cartmel Steeplechases Co.

Thos. Jekyl, Esq; Major of Dragoons; he shot himself at his Quarters in Canterbury.

The Lady Bellemont, Sister to the Earl of Grantham. By her death 15,000 l [pounds] devolved to the daughter of Sir Rob. Clifton, Kt of the Bath, her Ladyship's grand-daughter.

It is perhaps a pity that after 1867 the magazine underwent a modernizing facelift and there are fewer obituaries!

With the growing popularity of local newspapers from the mid-nineteenth century, we begin to see a growth in the number of regular 'Births, Marriages and Deaths' columns in the local newspaper, for which the newspaper owner or printer now began to charge. The costs of inserting an entry would usually have been within reach of most middle-class families. In 1876, for example, the *Clapham Observer* was charging one shilling for a domestic announcement. If you are in doubt as to whether an obituary was inserted by the printer as opposed to being paid for by the family then look through the paper to see if you can see a paragraph listing the price for insertion. If there isn't one it is likely the entry was inserted by the printer. Some entries merely state the name and date of death of the person, usually with their place of residence, and in some cases this was because the newspaper charged by the word, so many families kept the entries brief. The obituary for my great-great-grandfather in the Births, Marriages and Deaths column of the *Westmorland*

(Left) The obituary for James Dickinson, who died aged seventy-four, provides a splendid photo of him as a young man. (Author's collection)

Gazette simply reads: 'John Stewardson Dickinson died aged 68 at Hill Mill Tuesday 6th June 1881'. Apart from giving me the day of the week on which he died, this tells me nothing more than the information I have on the death certificate. The growing number of local newspapers being digitized and made available online means they are an increasingly useful short cut for locating deaths, not just before 1837, but for those we fail to find in the GRO death index. This will be especially useful for those that occurred after the last publicly available census of 1911. Usually we can narrow down a date of death to the ten-year period when an ancestor last appears in one census and fails to appear in the next, but after 1911 we cannot look to see if he is still alive in 1921 and it is often much harder to pinpoint the death in the index.

The mid-nineteenth century saw the development of professional news reporters and the introduction of full-length obituaries written by a third party rather than a family member. Depending on the newspaper these may be found as a separate news item headed with the name of the person who has died, or under a section entitled 'District Intelligence' or similar. An obituary written as a news item by a reporter will usually give far greater detail than those placed in the 'Births, Marriages and Deaths' column, and you may even be treated to a photograph of your ancestor too. As in the case of information inserted by the printer in early local papers, take what you read with a pinch of salt. The reporter relied on facts gleaned from friends and family, sometimes only on the day of the funeral itself, and these may not be accurate. Try and check any facts given in other sources where possible. It's also a good idea to note on which day of the week a newspaper was published, as this will have a bearing on when an ancestor's obituary appears. If your ancestor died on the day the paper was printed you will need to look at the following week's paper, but in some cases you may even find it appears a couple of weeks later if space was short. Many obituaries contain long lists of those people who attended the funeral. Take a close look at these to see if there are any potential relatives who do not feature on your family tree. The obituary for my relative James Dickinson named several people who turned out to be cousins from various different branches of the family.

If your surname is sufficiently rare, a search of the British Newspaper Archive at www.britishnewspaperarchive.co.uk using the surname only and restricting your search to 'family notices' and 'articles' may reveal the obituaries of more distant family members who do not yet feature on your tree. The information given in the obituary may be sufficient proof to confirm their relationship to you, but in others you may have to investigate further to see if there is a family link.

DEATH OF MR. J. W. WILSON

GROUNDSMAN AND GARDENER

Forty-three floral tributes and many letters from friends in many spheres in which he was prominent were received at the funeral on January 20th of Mr. John William Wilson, 41, Fencepiece-road, Barkingside, who died, aged 66, on January 14th.

He was well known in local cricket and was umpire for Ilford Parks C.C. to whom he was affectionately known as "Pop."

He was employed for 30 years by the Ilford Council, and was head gardener at the Isolation Hospital for some years.

Born at Twickenham, Mr. Wilson came to Ilford to take over the Old Blues sports ground at Fairlop and from there went to the Parks Department.

He was also well known for the good work he did as secretary of Barkingside H.S.A. and as secretary of the National Old Age Pensioners' Association at Barkingside.

He also did a lot of benevolent work as a member of the Buffaloes.

He was forced to retire two years ago through ill-health, and leaves a widow, five sons and three daughters.

The obituary for John William Wilson. (Author's collection)

Case Study: The Obituary of Will Wilson

Will Wilson was my great uncle and I found a copy of a newspaper obituary for him tucked inside his memorial card. It provided vital evidence in locating his birth certificate, but I had to use it with care!

Will Wilson was neither rich nor famous, yet he has a six-paragraph obituary, written by a reporter, in the local newspaper. This is no doubt because he was heavily involved in the local community in many ways. Apart from giving me an insight into his life and the esteem in which he was generally held, the obituary also gives his age and date of death and the fact that he left a widow and eight children. This was very important for identifying his birth certificate, which I had failed to find despite knowing when and where he was born. Finding the obituary showed me why; his name was actually John William Wilson! It was not accurate in regard to his place of birth, however, stating that he was born at Twickenham, whereas I knew from census returns he was actually born some 300 miles away near Cartmel in Lancashire. Had I relied on the obituary alone, I would never have found his birth certificate.

National Collections of Local Newspapers

The respective National Libraries of Scotland, Wales and Ireland all have extensive collections of newspapers for each country, while the British

Library (BL) in London holds a massive collection of newspapers for the whole of the UK and Ireland and also overseas newspapers. Both the BL and the National Library of Wales are currently working on major newspaper digitization projects.

Systematic collection of newspapers by the British Museum Library (BL's predecessor) began in the 1820s but it was not until the 1840s that a comprehensive collection of provincial newspapers began. There are, however, many pre-1840 provincial titles in the BL's newspaper collection, although sadly there were serious losses to the collection during bombing in the Second World War.

The majority of its newspaper collection is currently housed at its search room in Colindale in north London. You can see which titles it holds there by using its online catalogue at http://explore.bl.uk and selecting

---

Case Study: The Obituary of Eliza Lansdell

Despite the fact that Eliza came from a working-class background she had a lengthy obituary in the local paper, which proved to be a gold mine of information.

Frances Eliza Lansdell was born in 1847 and died in 1939. Her obituary can be found in the Kent and Sussex Courier, entitled 'Nonagenarian's Death at Hawkhurst'. In this case Eliza is newsworthy partly because of her age, but again because she spent much of her time helping others. Here we learn a fantastic amount of detail about her life, ranging from her father's name, where she was born, lived and worked to details of how she met her husband! Much of this information could lead on to further searches. There may, for example, be surviving records for the Lillesden Estate, while further searches in archive newspapers will probably reveal other entries concerning the family. We also learn Mr Lansdell's place of interment and date of death.

Mrs Frances Eliza Lansdell aged 92, of Rayne Cottage, Talbot-road, Hawkhurst died on Sunday. A daughter of the late Mr and Mrs Campany she was born at Cold Harbour, Hurst Green and when she was quite young her parents moved to Kent Bridge, Hawkhurst. For some years she was a member of the domestic staff of the late Colonel and Mrs Edward Loyd at Lillesden, Hawkhurst and while there became acquainted with her future husband, the late Mr H. Lansdell an employee in the Lillesden stables. Her father-in-law the late Mr William Lansdell, bailiff on the Lillesden estate was very successful in fattening livestock. The late Colonel Loyd presented him with a handsome cup for his success in showing the two best open sow pigs under 10-months-old at Rye cattle show in December 1864. On leaving Hawkhurst Mr and Mrs Henry Lansdell went to Swattenden, Cranbrook where Mr Lansdell died in November 1911 aged 71 and was buried in Cranbrook cemetery. Mrs Lansdell soon returned to Hawkhurst and for the past 28 years had occupied Rayne Cottage. This grand old lady maintained her faculties practically up to the last. She often visited her friends in the parish and spent many hours conversing and reading to those lying on beds of sickness. She was a mother of ten children and seven are still living. She attended church regularly and expressed a desire for her remains to be taken into Hawkhurst parish church for the funeral service and then conveyed to Cranbrook cemetery for internment.

The Rev C. Compton conducted the funeral service at the Parish Church on Wednesday.

There then follows a list of all mourners and details of the undertaker.

'Newspaper Library' from the drop-down box when you search. Pre-1801 newspapers and journals are housed at its St Pancras reading room and if you wish to see which titles are held there you will need to again go to http://explore.bl.uk/ but select 'Everything in this catalogue' when you search.

Colindale is due to close at the end of 2013, but by this time the BL aims to have placed over six million pages of newspapers on its online 'British Newspaper Archive' (BNA). This website is already up and running and is part of the BL's collaboration with online publisher Brightsolid to produce a massive online newspaper archive accessible to the general public. The collection includes two million pages previously digitized for its '19th Century British Library Newspapers Database' and the ten-year target is to hit a total of forty million pages. When Colindale closes those newspapers that are not digitized will either be available at St Pancras on microfilm or, if they have not been microfilmed, as hard copies which will have to be ordered in advance from the British Library's new storage facility in Boston Spa in Yorkshire for viewing at St Pancras. As of April 2012 the '19th Century British Library Newspapers Database' is still available as a separate database and in two different forms; one in the public domain for which you need to buy a day or week pass (http://news papers11.bl.uk/blcs), and the other as a collection made freely available for members of local libraries across the country that have subscribed to the collection. In this case library card holders can access the database for free via their library website and using their library card ID. At the moment, this database contains almost twice as many titles as the database available via the public website, although the missing titles, as mentioned above, are now on the new British Newspaper Archive website.

Brightsolid also have plans to launch an institutional version of BNA and a subscription version for schools. The BL also has its 17th and 18th Century Burney Newspapers Collection available online. This is currently separate from the other online collections and hosted by online publisher Gale Cengage. It is again accessible via subscribing local libraries. It consists of over a thousand seventeenth to eighteenth-century newspapers collected by scholar Charles Burney and is likely to be added to the BNA in due course.

The National Libraries of Wales, Scotland and Ireland

As I write the National Library of Wales is currently digitizing all of its newspapers and journals that are now out of copyright, which is generally those published in Wales up to 1911. When it is finished (expected the end of 2012) this will be a massive fully searchable database of over 700 different titles touching all corners of Wales. To view newspaper titles held at the library look in its catalogue at http://cat.llgc.org.uk.

The contents of the newspaper catalogue at the National Library of Scotland can be explored at www.nls.uk/collections/newspapers. Online at http://digital.nls.uk/broadsides it has 'broadsides', which were the forerunners to newspapers. At first printed on single sheets, broadsides carried official proclamations and announcements, while by the nineteenth century they had evolved to become the equivalent, in many ways, of today's tabloids. You may find accounts of any particularly newsworthy suicides there.

The National Library of Ireland has an online listing of Irish newspapers including those that from part of the Newsplan project at www.nli .ie/en/catalogues-and-databases-printed-newspapers.aspx. Although it currently has no digitization programme it is worth taking a look at a commercial site called Irish Newspaper Archives. This is a project aiming to completely digitize all of Ireland's historic newspapers and can be found at.www.irishnewsarchive.com/about.php.

Identifying and Locating Historic Newspapers

Digitization is clearly the way forward in making newspapers more accessible while preserving the originals, but as yet only a small percentage of local newspapers have been digitized. Therefore, once you have checked

Newspaper Collections Online

National/London Papers and Magazines

- The *London, Belfast* and *Edinburgh Gazette*: all available free online at http://www.gazettes-online.co.uk
- *The Times* Digital Archive via libraries: http://infotrac .galegroup.com/default. The first two years of the *Daily Universal Register*, as *The Times* was initially known, are available on Ancestry.
- *The Guardian* and *Observer* Archive: http://archive.guardian.co.uk
- *The Daily and Sunday Express* and *Mirror* from 1900: www.ukpres-sonline.co.uk/ukpressonline/open/services.jsp
- *The Scotsman* 1817 onwards: http://archive.scotsman.com/
- *The Gentleman's Magazine*: some editions available freely online as Google books or via the Bodleian Library of Internet Journals www.bodley.ox.ac.uk/ilej

Provincial and Overseas Newspapers

- British Newspaper Archive www.britishnewspaperarchive.co.uk
- 19th Century British Library Newspapers Database http://newspapers11.bl.uk/blcs
- National Library of Wales Newspaper Collection /www.llgc .org.uk
- National Library of Scotland Broadside Collection http:// digital.nls.uk/broadsides
- Irish Newspaper Archives involves the complete digitization of Ireland's newspaper heritage in an effort to convert this valuable data into accessible information. http://www.irishnewsarchive .com/about.php.
- www.ancestry.co.uk has a growing database of provincial newspapers and the Andrew's Index.
- www.old-liverpool.co.uk A collection of snippets from old Liverpool papers including many obituaries
- New Zealand papers online: http://paperspast.natlib.govt.nz/cgi-bin/paperspast.
- Australian resources online including some newspapers: http://trove.nla.gov.au

Many libraries subscribe to the 19th Century British Newspaper archive, *The Times* Online Archives and the *Illustrated London News*, while some also subscribe to the British Library's 'Seventeenth and Eighteenth Century Burney Collection', which consists of over 1,200 newspapers and pamphlets mainly published in London, but also in Ireland, Scotland and some English provinces.

what is online, you will still need to see what is available at the local record office or library; the latter will often hold the greater selection. You should also consider using the national collections of newspapers discussed above.

Although there are several modern-day newspaper listings such as *Willings Press Guide, Benn's Media* and various other online sources, you will find that most only list those newspapers currently in print while, even if you check with the local record office, they may not hold copies of all relevant titles. To identify *all* of the local papers that covered the area you want at the relevant time use *Local Newspapers 1750–1920* by Jeremy Gibson, Brett Langston and Brenda W. Smith (3rd edn, FFHS, 2011). This covers England, Wales, the Channel Islands and the Isle of Man, and not only tells you what was being published when, but also where the relevant newspaper can be consulted. You are advised to then follow up your findings with a telephone call to the relevant library or record office to double check they hold copies for the exact year you want and to see if you will need to book a place on a film reader in advance.

For Scotland there is an excellent guide by Joan Ferguson entitled *Directory of Scottish Newspapers* (National Library of Scotland, 1984) while the North Waterloo Academic Press publishes listings of historic newspapers for England, Wales, Scotland and Ireland.

The most comprehensive guides of all, however, are the reports published by the British Library as a result of the Newsplan project. This project aimed to list all historic local newspapers to be found in archives and libraries in the UK and Ireland, and to microfilm those most at risk. To carry out the project the UK and Ireland were divided into ten regions and there is a printed list of newspapers for each, while eight of the regions also have their own website. Most of these regional websites provide a searchable database that you can use to look for a title or for the name of the place you are interested in. You can access these at www.bl.uk/reshelp/bldept/news/newsplan/newsplan.html, while the printed guides are currently available at the British Newspaper Library in Colindale, North London (at St Pancras reading room from late 2013) and in many major public libraries, archives and local studies centres.

If you are at the British Library, Colindale then use the *Newspaper Press Directories* available there, which list full details of all newspapers and journals published each year. Another excellent starting point is to use the British Library's online catalogue http://explore.bl.uk to identify all journals and newspapers held there (many of which will of course also be found in local archives). This provides full details of all its newspaper collections, but does not provide access to the content of newspaper articles. Remember to restrict your search to items stored at British Library

Newspapers, Colindale, by selecting 'Newspaper Library' as described above. Searching by the keyword of the place or area you are looking for is often the most fruitful way to search.

Older printed books remain a good secondary source to identify relevant newspapers and are often available second-hand or as free books online, although in many cases you will not be able to ascertain the current location of the newspaper you require. *A Handlist of English Provincial Newspapers and Periodicals* by Geoffrey Cranfield (Cambridge Bibliographical Society) lists seventeenth-century local newspapers and is frequently found for sale second-hand, as are copies of *A Census of Newspapers and Periodicals 1620–1800* by R.S. Crane, F.B. Kaye and M.E. Prior, while John West's book *Town Records* (Phillimore, 1983) provides a fairly extensive guide based on the *Tercentenary Handlist of English and Welsh Newspapers* and supplemented by the British Library catalogue listing of 1975.

An excellent website for providing free online access to old publications is *The Internet Archive* which can be found at www.archive.org. Here you will find the following:

- *The Newspaper Press Directory* for 1922 (C. Mitchell and Co.) which includes the UK and overseas and provides complete listings of all newspapers by title, location and subject matter; thus useful if you are trying to locate a publication by its subject matter. It also lists starting dates but only covers newspapers still being published at that time.

- *The Tercentenary Handlist of English and Welsh Newspapers 1620–1919* (pub. *The Times*, 1920)

- *The Newspaper Press Directory* (published annually since 1846)

If you are lucky you may find that the contents of the newspaper you are interested in has been indexed, making it much easier to locate obituaries where you do not know your ancestor's date of death. To find out if any indexes have been compiled for your county of interest again use the guide by Gibson, Langston and Smith mentioned above or search the internet using a phrase such as 'Cambridgeshire newspaper indexing'. It's also worth contacting the record office in case any new local indexing projects are underway.

Further Online Newspaper Resources

There are many online collections of historic national papers, such as the *The Times* and *Daily Express*, available to the general public (See Newspaper

Collections Online). *The Times* digital archive will often be available via your local library website and is free to access for members of subscribing libraries. It is often worth considering a random search for your ancestor in such collections, depending of course on how common his name was. Even a small mention in the list of mourners at the funeral of someone well-known may reveal a new facet of your ancestor's life about which you knew nothing. If you are looking for the obituary of an ancestor who emigrated, a number of foreign press collections are now available online too.

The Andrew's Card Index was originally compiled by chancery agents between the 1880s and 1970 in order to help locate missing people in connection with unclaimed estates. It contains notices taken from newspapers and other official sources and is estimated to contain 70,000 entries: these include obituaries, notices relating to wills, unclaimed estates, and deaths abroad. Quite often the original newspaper cutting has been annotated with references from original wills, or with information from civil registration records. The index is available online at Ancestry or may be searched courtesy of the Institute of Heraldic and Genealogical Studies in Canterbury for a fee.

Tips for Locating Obituaries and Inquest Details

If you fail to find an inquest report or obituary as expected you may need to widen your search. The event you are looking for may not be found in the newspaper that was published closest to home. Local newspapers varied in their content and while one might carry full news stories, another might carry mainly adverts. When I was searching for an account of the death of a miner in an accident in Tilmanstone near Deal in Kent I found that the most local paper, the *East Kent Mercury*, made no mention of it because it mainly carried adverts. I had to go further afield to Dover library to look in the *Dover Express*, which carried much more news and featured a long article on the incident together with a full account of the inquest. Newspapers had different sized catchment areas too: while some concentrated on one particular town and its environs others, such as the *Westmorland Gazette* and *Hampshire Chronicle*, had county-wide coverage. Make sure you have checked all relevant papers and if any of your ancestors died away from home check both the local papers and the paper for the locality where they died.

Similarly, do not rule out a newspaper because of its title. You may find that a paper published in a town many miles away was used by your family to announce deaths, perhaps because it had a wide catchment area, followed politics they approved of, or because it was more prestigious. Thus *Jackson's Oxford Journal* has proved very useful for searching for references to my Heritage family who lived almost fifty miles away near Stratford-upon- Avon, despite the fact that Stratford had its own paper.

The beauty of using a digital newspaper collection such as the British Newspaper Archive is that you can search for a reference to a place or ancestor over the whole collection rather than in just one newspaper. This can sometimes turn up surprising results. When searching for a report of the death of my London ancestor John Perdue, who died from burns sustained after his smock caught fire, I could find no trace of a report in the local London papers, but a search of the BNA database brought up a short paragraph about his death in the *Liverpool Mercury*! He had no connections with Liverpool and this is a classic case of a distant provincial paper gleaning news from elsewhere because it thinks it is newsworthy.

Further Research

What you learn about your ancestors in the pages of the newspaper may well lead you to other death records such as certificates, gravestones and wills, but they can also open the way to opportunities for further research in a host of other records, such as employment records and records relating to societies or committees to which your ancestor belonged. This might include the local parish council, a church committee or the records of a friendly society. Records of church committees may be deposited at the local record office, as may the records of any friendly societies to which your ancestor may have belonged. Established in the eighteenth century, these were mutual aid associations which offered members insurance against sickness or old age. Members paid a subscription and in return received financial help for themselves and their families if they became ill and could not work, during old age, or if they died and still had dependent family members. Roger Logan's book *Friendly Society Records* (FFHS, 2000) provides an extremely useful history of the societies and description of the records you may find. He states that by 1803 an estimated thirty-eight percent of families were connected to a friendly society and by the early 1900s there were about 7,000 such societies in England and Wales. If an obituary shows that your ancestor was a member of the Freemasons, the Ancient Order of Foresters, Oddfellows, or the Royal Antediluvian Order of Buffaloes (Buffaloes), as was the case with Will Wilson, further information about him may be available in their records. The Freemasons have a museum and archive in London where records can be searched (www.freemasonry.london.museum/archives), the Oddfellows have a growing online archive collection (www.oddfellows.co.uk) and the Foresters' Heritage Trust (www.aoforestersheritage.com) accepts research enquiries and is currently indexing its collection.

You can also look out for newspaper announcements or news items concerning these groups locally which may have involved your ancestor.

Conversely you can often follow up information discovered through other death records in local newspapers. If your ancestor's will states that his property should be put up for sale after his death, then look for an auction notice in the local newspaper in the months after the will was proved. This should give further details of what the property was like and often who occupied it or was dealing with the sale. It may also state the name of your family's solicitor, which may lead you to a relevant collection of solicitors' papers that have been deposited in the record office.

Case Study: The Suicide of Thomas Heritage

Thomas Heritage, my great-uncle three times removed, committed suicide in 1904. The newspaper report of his inquest gives full details not only of how he took his own life, but considers his reasons for doing so. Revealed here is a story of constant ill health, pain and financial worry, no doubt some of the commonest reasons for people taking their own lives. The report builds a vivid picture of Thomas's life and the following is a transcription of the inquest report as published in the Stratford Herald *for 28 October 1904.*

Suicide of a Publican. Deep sympathy will be felt in Ettington for the widow and children of Mr Thos. George Heritage for many years landlord of the Saracen's Head, who was found drowned in a pond at Ettington Park on Tuesday morning, and on whose body an inquest was held at the Lord Nelson coffee house on Wednesday afternoon by Mr. G. F. Lodder, deputy coroner for South Warwickshire. Mr. Rainbow was chosen foreman of the jury.

Angelina Heritage, of the Saracen's Head, said the deceased was her husband, and he would have been 45 had he lived till Thursday. For the last eight years he had been in very bad health, suffering a good deal from eczema, brought on by rheumatism. It worried him a good deal. Dr Pitt formerly attended him, and latterly Dr Alexander, and he had been twice to a Birmingham specialist. Dr Alexander had attended him recently for eczema in the right foot. It did not prevent him getting about, but it must have given him pain to do so. Her husband was in financial difficulty. He had been at the Saracen's Head for seventeen years. The late Mr. Shirley was the owner, and she understood Flower and Son, Ltd. had taken it over until the son came of age. They had had notice to leave, which expired on September 29th, but that did not seem to affect him: indeed, recently he had seemed better

119

and brighter. She did not know why he got notice, whether it was because he did not do sufficient trade. Her husband was a temperate man, not given to excessive drinking. They had been staying on at the house to oblige the new tenant. The sale took place the previous day (Tuesday). They did not sell up everything. Deceased was about on Monday and helped to get ready for the sale. He did not lead her to suppose he was going to do away with himself. On March 27th 1900, he attempted to take his life by cutting his throat. There was no cause for his actions then beyond ill health. At two o'clock on the morning of Tuesday deceased passed through her bedroom fully dressed, and said he was going downstairs. Nothing else passed between them. As he did not return in a short while she got anxious and gave information to the police.

P.C. Arthur Sharp said at 4 a. m. on the 25th, from information left at his station that the deceased was missing from his home, he went out to make a search in the district and at 10.10 a.m., while looking round the fish-ponds in Ettington Park he saw the body in the water, three or four yards from the bank. The pond was about a mile from the Saracen's Head. He went for assistance from the gardens and got the body out. He examined it, but found no marks of violence. He also searched the body, but only discovered a pocket-knife and a few small articles. Deceased was fully dressed, with the exception that one boot was missing. The body was in a standing position, and the cap could just be seen above the water. He was quite dead, and there was frost on his cap. Witness removed the body to the Saracen's Head. He was called in previously when Heritage attempted to cut his throat, and there was no reason for that except that he had been ill and depressed. Witness had known him for 10 years, and lately he seemed more cheerful than usual.

Thomas Heritage, 16, son of the deceased, said his father slept with him on the night of the 24th. During the night he woke up and found his father was dressing. He asked what was the matter, and his father replied that he was just going downstairs. He often got up in the night. He never saw his father again.

By the jury: Witness noticed nothing strange in his manner.

The Coroner, in summing up, said there was nothing in the evidence to suggest that anyone was responsible for the death of the deceased other than himself, and there was no doubt that he got up in the night, walked to the pond, and committed suicide by drowning. He seemed to have had a certain amount of worry and to have been in a bad financial way. Very likely the fact that he was leaving the public-house where he had been for 17 years might have preyed on his mind, and led him to do what he otherwise would not have done. Probably they would come to the conclusion that he was not in his right mind.

A verdict of *Suicide while temporarily insane* was returned.

Chapter 6

WILLS AND OTHER PROBATE RECORDS

Wills are one of the most important sources in family history, adding substantially to our knowledge of the testator and his family and often confirming relationships we may have been unsure about from other records. They also provide an insight into our ancestors' lifestyles and sometimes even their personalities. Although relatively few wills survive before the mid-sixteenth century, some pre-date parish registers and enable you to add earlier generations to your family tree. By contrast, wills that are only a few months old may also be viewed by the general public, so this is an essential source throughout the course of your research.

Who Made a Will?

Generally speaking, anyone could make a will as long as they were over the age of twelve (for women) or fourteen (for men). In 1837 the minimum age was raised to twenty-one for all. Until the Married Women's Property Act of 1882, although a married woman could write a will, her husband was not legally bound to honour it if she predeceased him. This was because all her property legally passed to him at their marriage. Once a woman became a widow she regained control of any property she had and you will find many wills written by widows. The wills of prisoners, suicides, and of those considered to be insane were also not legally valid.

It has been estimated that about one in ten people left a will up to the nineteenth century when figures begin to rise.[1] Many people presume that their ancestors were not sufficiently wealthy to have left wills. Although it is true that wealthier people were more likely to have done so, there are many instances of humbler ancestors making wills too. Conversely a better-off ancestor may not have bothered to write a will if he knew his estate would be distributed as he wished after his death. You should routinely look for a will for *all* your ancestors, or else risk overlooking a potential goldmine of information about your family. We should also take care not to make assumptions about ancestors based on a modern interpretation of descriptions of them in historic records. During research into my family in Warwickshire I frequently encountered a man described as 'Thomas Heritage, labourer'. Despite this humble description, when he died in 1762 he left a will that showed he was actually a man of some wealth. Miriam Scott, writing in her *Index to Dorset wills and administrations proved in the PCC, 1812–1858* (Somerset and Dorset Family History Society, 1992), found that a large proportion of testators whose wills were proved in the Prerogative Court of Canterbury (PCC) were labourers. This is despite the fact that the PCC was the most important and expensive probate court in England and Wales.

What Can a Will Tell You?

The nature of a will means that the testator names the beneficiaries to whom he wishes to leave his estate after his death and these are usually family members. Wills are therefore one of our most important sources for building a pedigree. Many simply record the legacies of a parent to their children, whose names you may already know, but they will often provide information regarding the spouses of married daughters as well as details of more distant relationships. My ancestor Charles Chapman Heritage died in 1868 and in his will he named his 'cousin Charles Hemming of Mickleton, Gloucestershire' as one of several executors. Charles Hemming was unknown to me and so the will led to the discovery of a new branch of the family, while at the same time narrowing down the date of death for Charles Hemming, who had died by the time the will was proved nine years later.

The wills of spinsters and, to a lesser degree, bachelors, are extremely useful because they often name a long list of nieces, nephews, siblings, godchildren and friends, all of whom received bequests. Spinsters frequently played an important part in the lives of their siblings, living with the family and helping to run the household and bring up any children, while an older bachelor might well take on one of his nephews to succeed him in his business. So it is worthwhile studying the wills of any relations who remained unmarried, in order to get an insight into the wider family.

Case Study: The Will of Agnes Williamson, Spinster

Agnes was the sister of my ancestor Dorothy Williamson and died a spinster, aged seventy-six, in 1811. Her will was an eye-opener for me in many ways as it provided a much wider view of the family than the wills left by those of my ancestors who had direct descendants to leave their estate to. The following abstract summarizes the information to be found in the will.

Abstract of the will of Agnes Williamson of Gateside in Selside, in the parish of Kendal, Westmorland.[2]
Legacies to:

- Agnes wife of John Stewardson: niece. One bedstead, hangings, one feather bed, one pair of blankets, all wearing apparel, one bible and Hervy's Meditations in two volumes
- Dorothy Taylor, widow of Kendal: niece. £5
- Remainder and residue of estate to be divided between: Mr John Farrer of London, Agnes the wife of John Stewardson, Agnes the wife of John Wilkinson of Kendal and Dorothy the orphan daughter of Joseph and Jane Reynolds (in trust until she reaches 21 years)

Executors: John Farrer of London and John Stewardson of Selside
Witnesses: Thomas Airey and Robert Stephenson
Written: 19 April 1808
Proved:

- 23 March 1811 at the Archdeaconry of Richmond in the Diocese of Chester
- Estate worth under £800
- John Stewardson was the only surviving executor
- Note: Testatrix died on 5 or 6 January 1811

Agnes's will gave me vital clues as to what had happened to other family members. Her will told me that John Farrer (he was her nephew and was already on my tree) was living in London. This was the first indication that a branch of the family had moved 'down south'. John was named as an executor, but was dead by the time the will was proved almost two years later. I was able to locate his will on TNA's PCC wills online, which showed he was clearly a wealthy man and lived in Clapham. His will clarified some of the relationships that Agnes had left undefined. Both Dorothy Reynolds and Agnes Wilkinson were her great-nieces. Investigation on Family Search showed that Agnes's sister Jane had married Joseph Reynolds in 1780 and her sister Dorothy had married Thomas Taylor in 1787. I was able to learn more about John Farrer from Ancestry's London parish register collection. He and his sixteen-year-old daughter Julia were buried on the same day, leaving his son William and widow, Julia, behind them.

Agnes's will not only told me a lot about other family members, but it also showed that she was a pious and educated woman. *Hervy's Meditations* was a devotional text written by eighteenth-century clergyman James Hervey, while the fact that she lived a comfortable life is shown in her legacies of her feather bed and hangings, which were luxury items. Her place of residence is given as Selside and, since this is where her niece Agnes Stewardson lived, it is very likely that she lived with Agnes and her husband John.

Wills provide details of occupations and addresses, not just for the testator, but often for those named in the will. Addresses may show the location of a relative who had moved away from the family's home parish, while occupations and the nature of the goods and property mentioned will give an idea of the family's wealth and status; usually any real estate will be named or described too, helping you to envisage what it was like or even locate it on a map. Wills can also help pinpoint dates of death for the testator and occasionally an executor if he died in between the time the will was written and proved; the latter will be clear from the wording in the probate act at the foot of the will. Very importantly, the extra detail

The will of my ancestor William Holbrook, 1727. (Author's collection)

125

found in wills may help clarify and confirm entries in parish registers. This is especially helpful if your family regularly used the same first names, making it difficult to distinguish between the various branches of the family, or where you are researching a more common surname.

Case Study: Edward Dickinson – Using a will to verify a pedigree
It can be hard to trace a pedigree with certainty before 1837. Parish register entries may give insufficient detail for us to be sure we have found the correct baptism or marriage. Finding a will can provide the missing evidence.

My ancestor Edward Dickinson married Mary Stewardson in 1806 in Kendal, Westmorland and they settled in the nearby hamlet of Garnett Bridge. I found one potential baptism for Edward and this was in the parish of Hawkshead, to parents James and Elizabeth. Hawkshead is over twenty miles by road from Garnett Bridge, however, and I wanted further evidence to be sure that this was the correct baptism. There were also baptisms for three other siblings at Hawkshead and a further four baptisms, to what seemed to be the same couple, in another parish several miles away. Further evidence came in the form of the will of James Dickinson, written in 1808. This proved the link between the James and Elizabeth at Hawkshead and my Edward at Garnett Bridge because James also described himself as 'of Garnett Bridge', he named his wife as 'Elizabeth' and left legacies to eight children whose names matched the baptisms I had already found.

Probate and the Process of Making a Will

The processes involved in making a will have changed little over the centuries. After the testator's death the executors presented the will at the relevant probate court. If the court was content that the will was genuine and the executors were the people named in the will, it granted probate by issuing letters of probate to the executors and returning the will (or a copy of it) to them. Then a copy of the will was bound into a large register. These are known as 'registered' wills. Most courts charged an extra fee, on top of the probate charge, for registering a will and some of your ancestors may not have wished to pay this fee. In this case the will remained as an 'unregistered' will. Registering made it more easily accessible if anybody wanted to read it to clarify the contents: the majority of surviving wills are registered wills. Unregistered wills may be found among family papers, or occasionally a record office may have a separate collection of unregistered wills. A good example is at TNA where there are two sets of wills relating to the Prerogative Court of Canterbury. PROB 11 contains registered wills

Probate Terminology

- *Bona notabilia*: from Latin meaning 'notable goods' and denoting an estate worth more than £5 (or £10 in London).
- Codicil: an addition to the will made by the testator after the original will had been written.
- Common law: the law as derived from custom and judgments made in court, rather than from statutes passed by government.
- Executor: the person or persons appointed by a testator to carry out his wishes as stated in his will.
- Letters of administration: issued by a probate court to a next of kin or other person when there was no will. Letters of administration are often referred to as 'admons', an abbreviation of the word 'administration'.
- Letters of probate: issued by the probate court. Gave an executor authority to proceed with the administration of the deceased's will. Originally consisted of a copy of the will and a separate document containing the probate act. This was attached to the will or written at the foot of it.
- Probate Act: clause appended to the will by the probate court giving details of the date probate was granted, to whom, and how much the estate was worth. Up to 1898 this value did not include freehold land, unless it was leased out. It will be in Latin until 1733.
- Probate court: court that issued letters of probate. The process of applying for letters of probate is often referred to as 'proving' a will.
- Testator: someone who has made a will.

and PROB 10 original wills, including any that were not registered. Only PROB 11 is included on TNA's online will collection; PROB 10 must be searched at Kew.

Nuncupative and Holographic Wills

Although the great majority of wills were signed before at least two witnesses, 'nuncupative' wills were made orally before witnesses, usually as the testator was dying. The witnesses would later swear before the probate court that these were his true wishes. Nuncupative wills were not acceptable as a means of passing on land; only personal goods. They were also not accepted by the courts after 1838, unless made by a serviceman killed on active service. Whereas most wills were written by a third party on behalf of the testator (either a local villager or cleric who was literate, or a solicitor) 'holographic' wills were written out by the testator himself and were not witnessed at the time of writing. The will would later be presented to the court by witnesses (usually close family members), who could swear to its authenticity based on their familiarity with his handwriting and knowledge of what he wished to happen to his estate after his decease.

Where There Was No Will

In many cases an ancestor did not make a will and died 'intestate'. In this case there will often be no record of what happened to his property after his death. It would usually have passed to the spouse or have been divided among other family members. You may, however, find 'letters of administration'. These were usually granted to a next of kin, or sometimes a creditor if the deceased died owing money, and gave the person in question authority to administer the estate. The administrator would usually also have to sign an administration bond, agreeing to provide an inventory of the deceased's goods and to pay any debts owed. The bond had to be signed by two other people who stood 'surety' for the administrator and who would be liable for a hefty fine if he failed to carry out the requirements of the court in regards to the estate. Up to 1733 the first half of the bond was in Latin.

My relative Henry William Hemming Heritage was an innkeeper at Ettington near Stratford-upon-Avon and died intestate in 1881. At his death several tradesmen were owed money from the estate. His widow, Amelia, applied to the court for letters of administration, which were duly granted, and the debts owed are listed on the back of the letters of administration. These included payments to the local blacksmith, grocer and brewery, as well as doctor's fees. Although inventories were routinely required with wills up to 1782, the court would usually ask for an inventory of the deceased's goods to be made where letters of administration were granted after this date. In cases where a will was made but there was no surviving executor, the court would appoint a new person to administer the estate. In these circumstances you will find letters of administration attached to a will.

Inheritance Laws
A testator has not always had the right to decide who should inherit his estate, and the laws of property inheritance are complicated. The phrase 'will and testament' dates back to before the Norman Conquest when these were two separate documents. A will dealt with real estate (land and buildings) which was 'devised' to the appropriate heir. A testament dealt with moveable goods (often referred to as 'personalty'), which could be 'bequeathed' to whomsoever the testator

wished. Personalty included household goods, livestock, crops, debts, and also leases on houses or land where the lease ran for a set number of years. By Norman times both the will and testament were combined into one document known simply as a 'will' although the introductory phrase 'this is the last will and testament of . . .' was retained.

After the Norman Conquest in 1066 all real estate became the property of the king, who allowed his subjects the use of it in return for certain services. Originally a testator could not make provisions for passing on land by means of a will. The majority of real estate was subject to common law, which dictated how it should be inherited. In most parts of the country the eldest son inherited with a portion reserved for the widow. This was known as 'primogeniture'. In some areas different systems operated, such as 'Borough English' which was often found in Norfolk and designated that real estate should pass to the youngest son. In Kent a system known as 'gavelkind' was often found, where real estate was shared between all sons (or daughters if there were no sons) equally. If the testator wished to leave his land to someone else, perhaps a younger son, a common work-around was to set up a trust giving possession of the land to trustees who would hold it on behalf of the person whom a testator wished to inherit it.

From 1540 (after an Act of Parliament known as the Statute of Wills) the government began to relax the rules on the inheritance of real estate and from this date some real estate could be devised, providing the testator was over twenty-one and not a married woman. By the end of the sixteenth century there were very few restrictions on leaving real estate. Until 1540 you will see few references to real estate in wills, while those children who automatically inherited their father's estate may not be mentioned. There were also strict laws concerning the estate of those who died intestate. A widow was automatically entitled to a third of the estate and from 1670 the remainder had to be divided equally between any children. If there were none, it passed to any surviving parents, and then to siblings.

Interpreting a Will

The language of wills has changed over the years. Early wills are typically verbose, while later ones are usually comparatively concise. Before the eighteenth century there was almost always a lengthy preamble to the will, in which the testator commended his soul to God. Before the mid-sixteenth century many testators made bequests to the church in atonement for their sins and left money for masses to be said for their souls after death. The latter were specifically banned during the Reformation. Bequests of money to a distant church may indicate a testator's birthplace.

As you progress further with your research you will have to cope with reading older styles of handwriting. For tips on this refer to Chapter 2. Familiarity with the language used in wills will also help you to cope with reading them.

Many of the phrases used in wills were stock phrases and some of the terminology was designed to forestall an estate leaving the family under certain circumstances. Up to 1882, if a widow remarried then her new husband would own any property left to her under her previous husband's will. Therefore you will frequently see property left to the widow for the 'course of her natural life or until she remarries'. When she died, or if she remarried, the property would then pass to another family member. This was not designed to discourage a second marriage, but to prevent a new husband inheriting the estate instead of any children from her first marriage. Even where a testator had never written a will before you will still see the phrase 'I revoke all other wills.' This was a legal requirement so that no-one could bring forward a will of an earlier date and claim it was the valid will.

Where a child has not been mentioned in a parent's will or has perhaps been left a token few shillings, don't presume he has fallen out of favour with the testator. He may already have received his share of the estate in advance. Also bear in mind that a testator would often try and give away some of his estate before his death to reduce the value of his estate for probate and other fiscal purposes: so the property mentioned in his will may not have been everything he owned. Conversely, goods or property mentioned in a will may have been sold before he died. Although the probate act will give you an idea of how much his estate was worth, up to 1881 this was often reflected in terms of probate duty bands rather than an exact figure; from 1881 an exact value was given. Where appropriate, death duty registers will help clarify what was left when an estate was proved.

Terminology relating to family members has changed over the years and care needs to be taken when interpreting them, especially in early wills. Someone described as the 'natural' son or daughter of the testator was not necessarily illegitimate. It was only in the nineteenth century that this term started to be used for a child born out of wedlock. Before this it indicated a son or daughter by blood as opposed to a son or daughter-in-law, while the term 'in-law' could relate to any relationship formed through marriage, so a 'daughter-in-law' might actually be a stepdaughter.

It is sometimes possible to get an insight into our ancestors' personalities through reading their wills. Charles Chapman Heritage, mentioned above, was clearly a man who paid intricate, if not obsessive, attention to detail. In his nine-page will he stated exactly what should happen to each piece of property and each of his possessions; he even drew up his own inventory to accompany the will. This listed all his personal goods and furniture, item by item, including the contents of his inn and grocer's shop and his house; room by room and right down to the last sheet, spoon, lock and grate.

Case study: The Wills of Thomas and Margaret Sacre – Using Wills to Flesh out a 16th-Century Family Tree

Early parish registers can be frustratingly sparse in detail and many don't begin until the late 1500s. Wills often become crucial in order to continue a pedigree. I used wills to extend the family tree for various branches of the Sacre family of West Kent back to the early 1500s. The wills of Thomas Sacre of East Sutton and his widow Margaret of neighbouring Boughton Malherbe were very informative and enabled me to create a detailed pedigree for this branch of the family. They also clearly showed that Margaret and Thomas had two adult sons by the name of John.

Facts learned from the will of Thomas Sacre: written 1537 and proved 1539:[3]

    Place of residence: East Sutton
    Place of burial: Headcorn
    Daughters: Alice, Elizabeth, Joan
    Wife and executor: Margaret

In a typical sixteenth-century preamble to the will he gives a donation to the church for any tithes he has failed to pay during his life, he pays for masses to be said after his death and also makes a contribution to the mending of the local highway.

Facts learned from the will of Margaret Sacre: written and proved 1549:[3]

    Place of residence: Boughton Malherbe
    Place of burial: Boughton Malherbe
    Eldest son: John
    Two younger sons: John and William
    Daughters: Alice Wood, Joan Poste, Margaret Gemett and Elizabeth Irope
    Sister: married to Mr Mercer
    Grandchildren: Katherine Poste, Joan Poste, Margaret Poste and Andrew Poste
    Son-in-law: Thomas Wood
    Executor: George Hudson

By the time Margaret died her daughters were married and the will gives their married names and the names of several grandchildren.

We also have details of four children not mentioned in Thomas's will: Margaret, William and two sons called John. Thomas's will was written before the passing of the Statute of Wills in 1540 so his real estate would have passed automatically to his male heir. It is likely that he had already provided for the other children not mentioned in his will. Margaret's younger son John died shortly after her and his will added further family members to the tree.

Locating Post-1858 Wills in England and Wales

From 12 January 1858, all wills in England and Wales were proved by a system of secular probate courts or registries overseen by the Principal Probate Registry (PPR). All records of wills and administrations were combined in a central index. Locating a will in this period is normally straightforward for the period 1861 to 1966 when the index is available online at Ancestry. Outside this period you will need to have an idea when your ancestor died. This information can usually be found from sources mentioned elsewhere in this book. Up to 1911 you can also narrow down the search by using census returns, noting when your ancestor fails to appear because he has presumably died.

How to Access the Probate Registry Index

All wills and letters of administration are indexed by surname, forename and then by date of probate. You can usually expect to find a will or letters of administration within six months to two years of the date of death, although there are exceptions. If anyone challenged the will, probate may have been delayed by several years. The index itself is very informative, especially in its early years, giving details of the deceased's full name, date and place of death, when and where the will was proved (or letters of administration granted), the value of the estate, and the name of the executor(s). If a beneficiary died before the estate was finally sorted, further grants of probate might be made at a later date, and there may be a list of dates of death and names of heirs in the margin of the register book, along with the dates of second and further grants.

There are various places where you can access the probate index. Although Ancestry's index mentioned above provides the index between 1861 and 1966, there are currently some gaps in their collection within these dates. (See their website for further details). Microfiche copies of the index are available at TNA and at the IHGS up to 1943 and at SOG to 1930. District probate offices have partial copies, but it is important to check

HERITAGE Charles Chapman.

Effects under £1,500.

22 February.   The Will
(as contained in Writings marked A and B)
of Charles Chapman Heritage late of Aston
Cantlow in the County of **Warwick** Grocer
deceased who died 24 October 1868 at Aston
Cantlow aforesaid was proved at **Birmingham**
by the oaths of Henry Hemming of the Parish
of Claines in the County of Worcester Cattle
Dealer and Charles Heritage of Aston Cantlow
aforesaid Grocer the Son the surviving
Executors.

The entry in the probate index for my ancestor Charles Chapman Heritage.
(Copyright © Ancestry.com. All Rights Reserved)

exactly what they hold and whether they allow the public to search their records because access conditions vary. A full list of district probate registries can be found at www.justice.gov.uk.

The only place where you can currently view the complete index is at the Office of the National Probate Registry in First Avenue House, 42–49 High Holborn, London, WC1V 6NP. Here you can search the original volumes of the probate index. Grants of wills and administrations are in the same book and indexed by year from 1871 onwards. Before this date they are separated out into different volumes, so be sure to check both. From 1996 onwards the index is available to search via a computer database known as 'Probateman', which is accessible in the search room. There is also a computer database known as 'Willfinder' for wills and administrations from 1920 to 1995, but it is nowhere near complete, and if you fail to find what you are looking for you will have to revert to searching the books year by year.

The PPR has recently announced plans to launch its own complete online version of the probate calendars towards the end of 2012, as well as the digitization of 300,000 soldiers' wills which have not been included in the calendars before.

If you can't access the index yourself the Principal Probate Registry conducts searches on behalf of members of the public; if you know the date probate was granted and can't get to London to order a copy in person, you can apply by post. Up to date information on costs and how to apply can be found at www.justice.gov.uk/courts/probate.

Locating Pre-1858 Wills

Locating wills before 12 January 1858 is more complicated. Probate was granted by a hierarchy of church courts and a methodical approach to your search is needed to ensure that you check all of the courts where your ancestor's will is likely to have been proved.

The church may seem an unlikely organization to have authority to grant probate, but it has been involved in the running of secular life for centuries. If you read wills dating from the sixteenth century you will notice that the opening paragraphs are preoccupied with the testator recommending his soul to God; very much the realm of the church.

The determining factor as to where the will was proved was where the deceased owned property. This was not necessarily the same place as where he lived. It is an irony that you may not find out where he owned property until you find the will! Therefore the presumption has to be made, at least to start with, that he will have owned lands in the area where he lived.

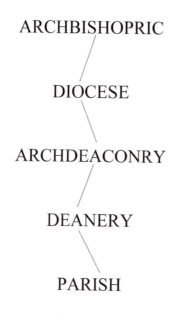

ARCHBISHOPRIC

DIOCESE

ARCHDEACONRY

DEANERY

PARISH

The church hierarchy

Familiarity with the administrative hierarchy of the church should help you understand the system of ecclesiastical courts that had probate authority prior to 1858. (Author's collection)

To understand the system of ecclesiastical courts and where your ancestor's will may have been proved, it helps to have an idea of how the church administration was, and still is, organized. Firstly it is divided into the two archbishoprics, or provinces, of Canterbury and York. The Archbishopric of Canterbury covers all of England south of the River Trent, and also includes Wales. The Archbishopric or Province of York covers all of England north of the River Trent (Cumberland, Westmorland, Lancashire, Northumberland, Yorkshire, Cheshire, Durham and Nottinghamshire.) Each is headed by its respective archbishop.

Both provinces are divided into dioceses, each headed by a bishop. The dioceses are further divided into archdeaconries, then into deaneries and finally into parishes. So the parish is the lowest unit of administration and the archbishopric (or province) the highest.

There were several types of ecclesiastical court which dealt with probate matters and they consisted of the following:

134

- Archbishopric courts (sometimes referred to as 'prerogative' courts)

- Diocesan courts (sometimes referred to as 'consistory' or 'commissary' courts)

- Archdeaconry or archidiaconal courts

The two Prerogative Courts of Canterbury and York were the most important and are often referred to as PCC and PCY respectively. The archdeaconry courts were the least important.

If your ancestor's estate was situated entirely in one archdeaconry, then his will is likely to have been proved at the local archdeaconry court. The fees would have been far lower than those charged by the higher courts. If your ancestor had property worth more than £5 ('bona notabilia') in more than one archdeaconry his will would usually be proved by a diocesan court. Similarly, if he held property worth over £5 in more than one diocese, the will would have been proved in one of the two prerogative courts, according to location of the property. If an ancestor held *bona notibilia* in both provinces, grants of probate would have been made separately for the parts of the estate in each archbishopric.

There are some exceptions to these rules. Even if your ancestor's estate was located solely in one archdeaconry his executors may have sought probate from a higher court because they thought it would be quicker, or because it was more conveniently located. It also gave greater privacy from curious neighbours who wanted to know how much was in the estate. If an estate contained government stocks then, between 1812 and 1858, it had to be proved at the PCC. This was because the Bank of England (which administered the stocks) would only acknowledge probate granted there.

In addition to these three types of probate courts there were also courts known as 'peculiars'. A peculiar was an area that did not fall under the jurisdiction of the local archdeacon or bishop for probate purposes. Probate jurisdiction was frequently under the control of an archbishop or bishop in a totally different geographical location, or sometimes belonged to the Dean and Chapter of a cathedral, a vicar or a manorial lord. The Dean and Chapter of St Paul's, for example, had probate jurisdiction over several parishes in the City of London, Middlesex, Essex and Hertfordshire, while at Cliffe in Kent the local vicar had probate jurisdiction. Many peculiars arose as a result of historic grants of probate jurisdiction by the monarch as a favour to individuals or institutions. The business of probate was lucrative, for fees were charged for every will that was proved, and so it was a useful way of rewarding faithful service to the monarch or for ensuring continued support. In medieval times many monasteries exercised probate authority. After the Dissolution of the Monasteries in the

1530s these lands were sold or given away by the king and their probate rights were often transferred to their new owners.

A Methodical Approach to Searching for a Pre-1858 Will

In pre-internet days, unless your ancestors were wealthy, it was logical to initially search the less important probate courts where your ancestor lived. Today we can take a slightly different approach to our research because there are now several will indexes online that can be swiftly checked before we start visiting record offices. An index to wills proved in the PCC is available on TNA's website. It's free and easy to search by either surname or place and it makes good sense to start here. If you are lucky enough to locate a will in the PCC you will have saved yourself hours of searching in the other probate courts and you can download the will for a relatively small charge.

Wills and Indexes Online

Below is a list of current online will indexes and websites.

One of the best sites if you are interested in probate records before 1858 is www.originsnetwork.com. It is divided into three sections: British Origins, Irish Origins and Scots Origins and various types of subscription are available. Scots Origins is free but mainly contains articles on Scottish genealogy and the IGI.

British Origins provides the 'National Wills Index' consisting of the following:

• Archdeaconry Court of London Index	1700–1807
• British Record Society Probate Collection	1320–1858
• Cheltenham Probate Abstracts	1660–1740
• Gloucester Wills Index	1801–1858
• Hertfordshire Will index	1414–1857
• Kent Probate Index	1571–1857
• Oxfordshire Will Index	1516–1857
• Prerogative and Exchequer Courts of York Probate Index	1688–1858
• Somerset Wills Abstracts	1385–1556
• Surrey and South London Will Abstracts:	1470–1858
• Surrey Peculiar Probate index	1660–1794
• York Medieval Probate Index	1267–1500
• York Peculiars Probate Index	1383–1883

Irish Origins provides the following:

• Dublin Will and Grant Books	1270–1858

- Index to Irish Wills   1484–1858
- Phillimore and Thrift Index to Irish Wills   1536–1858
- Sir Arthur Vicar's Index to the Prerogative Wills
  of Ireland   1536–1858

The National Archives www.nationalarchives.gov.uk
- PCC wills   1384–1858
- Death Duty Records   1796–1811
- Wills of Royal Naval Seamen   1786–1882

Findmypast.co.uk
- Bank of England Will Extracts   1717–1845
- Chester Wills and Probate   1492–1911
- London Probate Index   1750–1858
- PCC will index   1750–1800
- Northamptonshire and Rutland Probate Index   1462–1857
- Prerogative Court of Canterbury Wills Index   1750–1800
- Suffolk Testator and Beneficiary Indices   1847–1857
- West Kent Probate index   1750–1858

Other Websites
- www.kentarchaeology.org.uk

Indexes to medieval & Tudor Kent PCC & Canterbury Consistory Court wills
- www.scotlandspeople.gov.uk

Scottish wills 1513–1901
- http://cat.llgc.org.uk/cgi-bin/gw/chameleon?skin=profeb&lng=en

Pre-1858 Welsh wills
- http://history.wiltshire.gov.uk/heritage

A detailed catalogue of wills held in Wiltshire and Swindon Archives between 1540 and 1858
- http://genuki.cs.ncl.ac.uk/DEV/DevonWillsProject

Devon Wills Project
- www.essex.sturnidae.com/WillBen.htm

Essex Wills Beneficiaries Index 1675–1858
- www.ancestry.co.uk

A growing number of probate databases for the UK including some Irish and Scottish collections and the post-1858 National Probate Index between 1861 and 1966 (although there are currently some gaps within these dates).

The number of online will indexes is increasing regularly so it is worth keeping an eye on the 'What's New' sections of the various websites.

Despite the growing number of online will indexes you will still have to search for the majority of wills at local record offices. Since most wills were proved at archdeacons' courts, it makes sense to check these first, followed by the consistory courts and then, if your ancestors lived north of the River Trent, the wills of the Prerogative Court of York. These are held at the Borthwick Institute in York (which is part of the University of York) and there is an index for 1731–1858 at www.britishorigins.com. For up to date details of how to obtain copies or search the index outside these dates see www.york.ac.uk/library/borthwick.

Locating the correct record offices when you are searching for wills takes care because the boundaries of some dioceses may not coincide with the county boundary. South Warwickshire wills, for example, are found at Worcester record office because they are in the diocese of Worcester.

One of the best guides for pinpointing the location of wills is *Probate Jurisdictions: Where to Look for Wills* by Jeremy Gibson and Else Churchill (5th edn, FFHS, 2002). This is a very reasonably priced book and will tell you not only which courts you need to check, but also in which record office they will be found. *The Phillimore's Atlas and Index of Parish Registers,* edited by Cecil Humphery-Smith, also shows probate jurisdiction boundaries on its county maps, although it highlights only the lowest courts in each area and does not give the detail provided by Gibson.

Many record offices have created their own will indexes. These are arranged alphabetically by surname and are occasionally available via their online catalogue. In some cases you will have to search through calendars of wills held at the record office. Unlike indexes, calendars provide a partial index, being organized by the initial letter of the surname and then ordered by year or groups of years. Many record offices have microfilmed their wills for public viewing, but in some cases you will need to order the originals.

The majority of Welsh wills will be found at the National Library of Wales, although be aware that if your ancestor lived in the Welsh marches then you may find their will in neighbouring English probate courts. Welsh wills are available online at the National Library of Wales website.

Printed Indexes

Many will indexes and calendars have been published by societies such as the British Record Society, the Lancashire and Cheshire Record Society, the Yorkshire Archaeological Society and the Surtees Society. These will note whether the surviving document is a will or letters of administration and many academic libraries hold copies of these publications. Plenty of will 'abstracts' have been published too. Abstracts are where the information from a will has been extracted and summarized. This would typically include all details of the testator, beneficiaries, witnesses, executors and legacies, as well as when the will was written, where and when it was proved, and the value of the estate. The beauty of abstracts is that you can see all the relevant information at a glance, without having to wade through the legalese of the document. For an example, see the case study of Agnes Williamson on pages 124–125.

The Andrews Index, mentioned in detail in Chapter 5, includes some references to wills, while you may also find details of wills in both national and local newspapers, albeit usually only in relation to the higher classes of society.

Many wills for Devon, Somerset and Cornwall were destroyed during bombing in the Second World War but great steps have been taken to make up for this loss, notably the Devon Wills Project. This is a growing data-base that includes information from all published or publicly available sources of information about Devon wills, administrations and in-ventories. In recognition of the loss of West Country wills, the government preserved all copies of wills for Cornwall, Somerset and Devon made for death duty purposes between 1813 and 1857 (those for the rest of the country were destroyed to conserve space).

Between 1717 and 1791 all Catholics had to register bequests of land at the local Quarter Session Courts and, if you have Catholic ancestors, these provide a further source when looking for a will. Quarter Sessions records are in county record offices, while there were also some registrations at the Exchequer Court; these will be at TNA.

Problems Locating Wills

Although your ancestor may have written his will many years before he died, it is the date that the will was proved which will be recorded in the indexes you will use to find it, and therefore, unless his name was sufficiently rare, it helps to have an idea of when he died.

Until recently there was no legal obligation for a will to be proved and even today the smallest estates do not have to go through the probate process. If a will was not proved then there is unlikely to be any record of it, unless it survives among family papers or among solicitor's collections which have been passed on to a record office.

If your ancestor was of humble origin you may feel there is little point in checking the records of any but the archdeaconry court. However, exceptions abound in probate law. Any court might be temporarily closed, forcing executors to seek probate in a higher court, while you may be unaware that there was a peculiar court that had authority in the vicinity. In some places there was no archdeaconry court and the lowest court was that of the diocese. It is very important to know which courts had jurisdic-tion in the relevant locality and were operating at the time your ancestor died. The frustrating thing is that you may have to carry out extensive searches only to come to the conclusion that he did not leave a will.

Some estates were located entirely outside the area where the testator lived. It was quite possible for an ancestor to own land or property in another county; perhaps he had inherited it from another relative but never lived there himself, or had moved away at a later date. All probate courts have what are known as 'stray' entries too. These occurred where the executor lived a long way from the estate and was unable to travel to the local probate court. In this case he might take out a grant of probate at his own local court. Therefore it pays to keep an open mind as to where your ancestor's will may have been proved and to search the records of as many courts as possible.

Some early probate courts appear to have been peripatetic (they sat in different locations at different times) and this might result in a delay in probate being sought until the court was in the locality.

If you are looking for a will during the Commonwealth period you may struggle. Between 1646 and 1653 the majority of probate courts ceased business following Parliament's abolition of the Episcopacy. A new probate court entitled the 'Court for the Probate of Wills and the Granting of Administrations' was formed in 1653. This covered the whole of England and Wales, but ceased functioning with the restoration of the monarchy in 1660. Its records were amalgamated with those of the PCC and for this period means records of nearly all wills will be found amongst those of the PCC. In some cases, however, probate was postponed and estates simply administered without it!

Springboards to Further Research

Wills often lead the researcher to other records that provide further information about a family. They may mention a place of burial, which in turn leads to a memorial inscription, or may make reference to a piece of land or building. The latter may lead to the discovery of title deeds and leases, which often provide a wealth of genealogical details, especially where the property remained in one family for several generations. Where they survive, title deeds and leases may be found at the local record office, while some remain in the custody of the owner of the property if it still stands. Wills may also mention life assurance policies (see Chapter 4 for further details).

It is a very useful exercise to read the wills of any testators sharing your ancestor's surname and dying in the area where your family lived as they may well be related. Similarly your family may be mentioned as executors or beneficiaries in the wills of people who were friends or relations but did not share the same surname. Although these may be harder to identify, there are a few local indexes listing the names of beneficiaries, such as those for Suffolk and Essex (see 'Wills and Indexes Online'). It is worth checking with the local record office to see if any others exist.

Not all wills passed smoothly through probate and some were challenged by family members. The executor might also later be taken to court, accused of dishonesty in distributing the estate. Before 1858 such disputes would usually end up in either an ecclesiastical court, such as the Prerogative Court of Canterbury or, if it involved freehold property, the Court of Chancery. Court cases produced reams of paperwork and usually included written witness statements ('depositions') from family members and others. These shed light on family relationships, occupations and addresses, providing information that is not to be found elsewhere, as well as giving an insight into whatever the quarrel was about. Chancery Court records are at TNA and a growing number have been indexed; therefore it is worth searching for the surname in TNA's online catalogue. There may even be a note after the probate clause that indicates the will was disputed. Also look at www.origins.net, which has an Inheritance Disputes Index 1574–1714 listing cases that went to the Court of Chancery.

After 1858 records of disputes in probate cases do not routinely survive. TNA has a small sample of records for contentious cases between 1858 and 1960. These are found in J 121 and J 90 and are searchable online.

For further information on disputed wills, see TNA's online research guide 'Wills and Probate: further research'.

Inventories and the value of estates

Up to 1782 every executor or administrator was required to make an inventory of the deceased's goods. Real estate was not included in an inventory, but passing references may be made. After 1782 an inventory may be found if it was requested by an interested party in connection with the will. This would be lodged with the probate court where it would either be filed together with the will, or kept in a separate collection containing only inventories.

Since inventories of household goods were frequently compiled on a room-by-room basis, they can give you an idea of what your ancestor's house was like, not just in terms of what possessions your ancestor had, but also the number of rooms and layout of his house.

A succession of inventories can show how a family's material possessions increased or shrank over the years, as well as enlightening us about the types of household objects our ancestors used in their daily lives.

Case Study: The Holbrooks – learning about a family from wills, inventories and administration bonds

If your surname is not too common, then a search of local will indexes may add new generations to your tree almost instantaneously and, unlike parish registers, prove the link between them beyond doubt. Surviving inventories will also give you an idea of your family's wealth and status and list items used in their everyday lives and occupations.

My ancestor Margaret Holbrook was baptized in 1720 at Norton Lenchwick near Worcester to Lydia and Henry Holbrook. A search of the Worcestershire wills index at the record office revealed several grants of probate and administration to people with this surname in

The administration bond of my ancestor Henry Holbrook, dated 1721.

the area and, by reading through them all, I learned a lot about my family. Firstly, there was an administration bond issued to Lydia after Henry's premature death in 1721, after just four years of marriage.

An inventory of the goods of Henry Holbrook, 1721.

This accounted for the fact that there were no further children baptized after Margaret in 1720. On the bond Lydia swore to administer the estate fairly and to provide an inventory of all Henry's goods. 'William Holbrook' and 'Matthew Edwin' also signed the bond to stand surety that she would do this.

I also found a will and an administration bond relating to two men by the name of William Holbrook, both granted on 19 March 1727, indicating they had died within a very short space of time.

The will related to William Holbrook senior and he wrote it in August 1727, some seven months before it was proved (remember the New Year began on 25 March at this point). He was clearly Lydia's father-in-law, because he made bequests to his 'daughter-in-law Lydia Holbrook' and her children Thomas and Margaret. This meant I knew beyond doubt that the name of Henry's father was William, while he also mentioned his son 'John', who was therefore Henry's brother.

The administration bond related to 'William Holbrook junior' and he turned out to be William's son too, because administration was granted to' his brother John'. The fact that William senior did not mention his son William in his will may mean that William was already dead by August 1727 when he wrote it, but that a grant of administration for William junior was not sought until the ecclesiastical court was in the area or because the local court had been temporarily closed. Alternatively it may be that William had already received a share of the estate.

The inventories that accompanied each of the three grants provided an interesting insight into the lives of the Holbrook family.

The Inventory Accompanying the Administration Bond of Henry Holbrook 1721

There were two copies of this; one clearly copied out later by a different person who used different spelling. The inventories show how it is important to keep an open mind regarding spellings in historic documents. The use of 'on' instead of 'one', and 'tow' for 'two' can be very disconcerting for a modern reader. Reading a word aloud as it is spelled often gives a clue as to its identity! The meanings of some words are unfamiliar to us today and you will need to use a book such as Stuart Raymond's Words from Wills and Other Probate Documents (Federation of Family History Societies, 2004) to find out what they mean. In the inventory on page 143, for example, a 'meshfat' or 'mashfat' was used in the process of brewing. In this extract, taken from the inventory of Henry's estate, I have added modern spellings of any words that may not be obvious in brackets.

	£	s	d
Seven cowse [cows] on [one] Earlin [yearling]	16	10	0
For five Horses on Earlin Colt	22	0	0
On wagon two muckarts [muck carts] and other od [odd] implements	01	0	0
For wheat and maind [possibly maize] corn	15	0	0
For Barly [Barley]	17	10	0
For Pease and fetches [vetches]	07	5	0
For money in Pocket and werin [wearing] apparel	05	0	0
In the kitchin on furnise [furnace] on meshfat & other things	0	15	0
In the Dayery [dairy] howse [house] two pigs in salt on store pig one cheese press and other od things	03	15	0
In the Buttery on malt mill and for [four] Barrels	01	10	0
In the Little Chamber one bed and blanquets	00	10	0
In the hall Brass and peweter on Cubbard Stooles and cheerse [chairs] and other od things	02	0	0
In the parlor two beds and tow Bedsteds on table tow Cheests and Linnin	03	15	0
For five sheep and three Lames [lambs]	01	0	0
For the wheate cast and sown upon the ground	06	0	0
	109	10	0

The names of the 'Appraisers' Mathew Edwin and John Haines are written at the bottom. These were the people who conducted the inventory and were usually trustworthy locals.

The Probate Act Book

This was a chronological account of the business of a probate court. It recorded all wills that went to probate, as well as grants of administrations, and later grants where an heir came of age. It may provide extra details about both testator and executor that do not appear in the will. These may include references to current and former addresses, occupations and also marital status and relationships. Act books are especially useful where you believe there is likely to have been a will but it was not registered; you should find details of it in the act book. Likewise if someone held property abroad, although the PCC had probate authority, a reference may be found in the act book for the appropriate local court. Some courts had separate 'Administration Act Books' to record grants of letters of administration.

Death Duty Registers

From 1796 to 1903 death duty registers (DDR) are an extra source of information about the estates of our ancestors. This term actually covers three different types of taxes imposed on the estates of deceased people at different times: legacy duty, succession duty and estate duty. The death duty registers include brief abstracts of all wills or administrations subject to the tax. The importance for the family historian lies in the detail they provide concerning the deceased and his next of kin, and the fact that by 1857 most estates were subject to the tax (any estate worth over £20). Although taxes were rarely collected where the estate was valued at less than £1,500, there will still be an entry in the register. The registers also record which court granted probate, thus providing a short cut for locating a will, and indicating how much the estate was worth at time of death. This may be quite different to the value of the estate when the testator wrote the will. An entry will typically include the occupation and address of the deceased, names of the major beneficiaries, their relationship to the deceased (this can be useful for discovering the married names of daughters), the names of executors and, in some cases, notes regarding the dates of death of beneficiaries or the birth of posthumous children.

Death Duty Registers: points to note

- Before 1805 real estate and leasehold land were not subject to duty. Freehold land became liable in 1853.

- Many registers for the 1890s were destroyed by fire. These are shown as 'wanting' in TNA's catalogue.

- No duty was levied if the deceased lived abroad (1796–1903) or died in the service of his country.

- There was no duty on estates passed between spouses, children, parents or grandparents of the deceased up to 1805. After this the exemption was limited to spouse and parents and to spouses only in 1815.

Death duty registers are housed at TNA (class IR 26 with an index in IR 27). Those for what are known as the 'country courts' (non-PCC wills) are available as digitized images on TNA's website up to 1811. After these dates and for PCC wills you need to visit TNA in person. Further guidance is given in their online research guides to death duty records. IR 27 is available online at Findmypast and provides a useful index of all wills that were subject to death duties up to 1903. After this date a new system of recording duty paid was used and the files do not generally survive.

Case study: George Stewardson – Death Duty Extract 1807

One of the rarer surnames in my family tree is 'Stewardson' and, in an attempt to shed further light on my own branch of the family, I decided to study any online references to Stewardsons in TNA's online collections. I found an entry for a George Stewardson in the death duty extracts for 1807.

The death duty extract for George named four of his children as his beneficiaries. The inclusion of their names meant I was able to identify him as the George Stewardson who was a Quaker and who frequently appeared in the Quaker registers available online at the Genealogist and BMD Registers. These showed that George was born in 1720 in Shap, Westmorland, and married Dorothy Benson in 1761. They had six children and the fact that there was no mention of Dorothy or two of the children in the death duty extract suggested that they had died before he wrote his will. This was confirmed by further research in the Quaker registers.

Abstract of the death duty register relating to George Stewardson:

Date of the Probate: 7 January 1807

Value of Estate: Under £1000

Name and description of Testator: George Stewardson of Kendal, Westmorland Draper and Clogger

Name and Place of Abode of Executor: Simon Crosfield, Gentleman. Isaac Rigg, Cardmaker, both of Kendal.

Legatees: Thomas Stewardson, son; Deborah, Ann and Dorothy Stewardson, daughters

Executors to sell testator's real estate and the money from this to pay his debts and also a legacy of £200 to his son Thomas. The residue of money from the sale and also his personal estate to go to his three daughters Deborah, Ann and Dorothy.

With the information from the extract I was easily able to locate George's will[5] and compare the information in it to that in the DDR. Although the extract gives plenty of information about George and his family, the actual will fleshes this out. For example, it shows that Dorothy was to be offered first refusal to purchase George's shop in Stricklandgate Kendal, followed by her sisters Deborah and Ann jointly. If none of them wanted to buy the shop, it was then to be put up for general auction and the proceeds shared.

Irish Wills

The Irish probate system is very similar to that in England. Up to 1858 probate was granted by the courts of the Church of Ireland, although there were no archdeaconries. This means that the lowest courts were the diocesan or consistory courts. The Prerogative Court of Armagh was the highest court of probate and, if a testator held lands worth over £5 in more than one diocese, then his will would be proved there. Many Irish ancestors held land in England as well as Ireland and, in that case, the will was proved in the Prerogative Court of Canterbury.

In 1858 probate authority was transferred to civil courts headed by the Principal Registry in Dublin and in 1922 a Principal Registry was also formed in Belfast to serve Northern Ireland.

The great difference between searching for wills in Ireland and the rest of the UK is the tragic loss of records as a result of the fire at the Public Record Office in Dublin in 1922. This means that a substantial proportion of the original probate records before 1922 were destroyed. The calendars of wills and administrations compiled annually after 1858 do survive, however, and can be found both at the National Archives of Ireland (NAI) in Dublin and at the Public Record Office for Northern Ireland (PRONI). Although they do not make up for the loss of so many wills, they do provide much information: the name, address and occupation of the deceased, the place and date of death, the value of the estate, and the name and address of executors. Prior to Partition these calendars covered the whole of Ireland.

PRONI has a useful guide to the history of Irish probate records at www.proni.gov.uk/index/search_the_archives/will_calendars. Here you will also find images of calendar entries from 1858 for Armagh, Belfast, and Derry. These currently cover 1858 to 1919 and 1922 to 1943. Part of 1921 has also been added, with remaining entries for 1920-1921 expected to be added shortly. You can also view digitized images of actual will copies, which were made by the District Registries (and not affected by the fire), for the period 1858 to 1900, while this collection is shortly to be extended to include wills up to 1950.

NAI has placed Republic of Ireland calendar entries online at www.nationalarchives.ie/genealogy1/genealogy-records/wills-testamentary-records. These cover the period 1923 to 1982, although it is not the easiest database to use. Irish genealogist Chris Paton has placed some very helpful shortcuts to the calendars online at http://britishgenes.blogspot.co.uk/2012/03/southern-irish-probate-calendars-direct.html. Earlier calendars are soon to go online both at NAI and Family Search. NAI has a useful general introduction to wills on its website in its 'Genealogy/Genealogy records' section.

Surviving original post-1858 wills are held in the respective record offices, according to the location of the relevant probate court. *Probate Jurisdictions: Where to Look for Wills* (mentioned earlier) is the definitive guide. The will extracts recorded by Sir William Betham include many wills up to 1800 and are another vital resource. The extracts contain much genealogical information and are at NAI, with later copies at PRONI, while pedigrees based on the abstracts are available at the Genealogical Office located in the National Library of Ireland.

Much hard work has gone into reconstructing the information lost in the original wills from other sources. Sites such as Findmypast Ireland (findmypast.ie) Ancestry and Irish Origins (www.irishorigins.com) offer many Irish will collections. Familyrelatives is particularly strong in the number of Irish probate records it offers; this includes the 'Quaker Records Dublin Abstracts of Wills' collection, and these entries often include far greater information than those found in many other will abstracts or indexes, such as details of other relatives and burial places.

Major Sources for Irish Wills

- Index of Irish Wills 1484–1858, lists all the surviving wills at the National Archives of Ireland.
- Dublin Will and Grant Books Index 1270–1858.
- Phillimore & Thrift, *Indexes to Irish Wills 1536–1858* contains entries for many wills proved in the diocesan consistorial courts of Ireland up to 1800 with a few entries up to 1858.
- Vicars' Index to the Prerogative Wills of Ireland, 1536-1810. Index of all wills proved at the Prerogative Court of Armagh. Provides the name, residence, occupation or rank of the testator and date of probate.
- Betham's Index to Irish Pedigrees.
- The Society of Genealogists has a good collection of Irish will transcriptions. Search its catalogue at www.sog.org.uk.

Also see the box on Wills and Indexes Online.

Scottish Wills

Scottish ecclesiastical and legal history has developed quite differently from the rest of the UK and there are notable differences to be found when using Scottish probate records for research.

From about 1560 up to 1823 probate matters were dealt with by civil courts known as 'commissary courts'. Between 1823 and 1830 the power to 'confirm' wills (the same as granting probate in England) was transferred to the Sheriffs' Courts. Where the deceased left a will, the court issued what was known as a 'testament testamentar'; the equivalent to

English letters of probate, while if he died intestate it granted a 'testament dative'; the equivalent to English letters of administration.

Whereas in England, Wales and Ireland real estate could be devised from the sixteenth century onwards, this was not the case in Scotland until 1868. Before this time real estate was inherited according to the principles of primogeniture already discussed, and Scottish wills concerned only moveable goods. Even then, two-thirds of moveable estate was legally reserved for a man's widow and children, leaving him with only the remaining third to bequeath elsewhere.

All testaments and inventories up to 1901 are available to view at ScotlandsPeople. The index is free to search and there is currently a fee of £5 to download an image, irrespective of document length. Testaments after 1901 are held at the National Records of Scotland (NRS), except for last ten years where they will still be at the local sheriff's court. You can check the annual index of testaments known as the 'Calendar of Confirmations' from 1902 to 1996 at NRS in Edinburgh or at the Mitchell Library in Glasgow (to 1936). This covers the whole of Scotland and provides details of the deceased, place and date of death, and where their testament is recorded. The ScotlandsPeople Centre also provides access to digitized copies of the calendars. Women will be indexed under their maiden name and cross-referenced to their husband's surname.

Just as the Prerogative Court of Canterbury in England was responsible for proving wills where someone held land outside the country, so the commissariat of Edinburgh was responsible for confirmation where a person lived abroad. It also had ultimate jurisdiction for probate over the whole country.

The Service of Heirs

Although the inheritance of Scottish land followed strict rules of primogeniture, any heir who held land directly from the crown was required to confirm his identity, and thus his right to inherit, by presenting himself before an inquest presided over by local landowners. They would confirm he was indeed the true heir and make a 'retour' (return) of their findings. This was recorded in the Chancery Court. The original records are held at NRS and can be found from 1520 to 1847. Records will name the heir and his relationship to his predecessor and will be in Latin until 1847. Indexes are available at NRS from 1530 and the Scottish Genealogical Society (www.scotsgenealogy.com) has published CDs containing a summary of the retours for 1530 to 1699 and an index of retours 1700–1859.

When searching for a retour be aware that many heirs did not bother to go through this process until they wished to sell their property, so the entry may be many years after they actually inherited.

It is also worth looking at the Registers of Sasines for any lands that were transferred either through inheritance or sale. Any such transfer had to be entered into the Registers of Sasines and these can be consulted in Edinburgh or at local county archives. For further information see Chris Paton's blog of 11 February 2012 entitled 'Land Inheritance in Scotland' at http://walkingineternity.blogspot.co.uk.

Chapter 7

MISCELLANY

Some records do not merit a whole chapter to themselves, while other sources can provide useful details relating to an ancestor's demise, despite the fact that they are not primarily concerned with details of his death.

Memorial Cards, Funeral Papers and Post-Mortem Photographs

In our haste to research our family tree we can overlook the fact that various family papers may lie long forgotten in our attics or those of other family members. Many of these will relate to the deaths of family members and provide vital clues and short cuts for your research: the discovery of a death certificate will also save the cost of buying a modern copy!

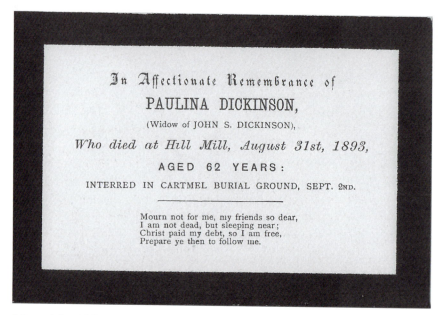

In Affectionate Remembrance of
PAULINA DICKINSON,
(Widow of JOHN S. DICKINSON),
Who died at Hill Mill, August 31st, 1893,
AGED 62 YEARS :
INTERRED IN CARTMEL BURIAL GROUND, SEPT. 2ND.

Mourn not for me, my friends so dear,
I am not dead, but sleeping near ;
Christ paid my debt, so I am free,
Prepare ye then to follow me.

Memorial card for my ancestor Paulina Dickinson. (Author's collection)

In the family archive you may find memorial cards (frequently referred to as 'funeral cards') and funeral papers, both of which are extremely useful and interesting sources. Memorial cards were printed cards sent to family members and friends after a funeral. They were very popular in the late nineteenth and early twentieth century and most contain the person's name, date of death, age and details of where he was buried. They often

Funeral papers of Emily Heritage. (Author's collection)

also include a verse which, although highly sentimental, may give an indication of the person's character or the cause of death. These verses were probably chosen by the family from a list supplied by the undertaker or printer. That for my uncle, who died as a baby, matched the verse on his gravestone. Memorial cards are very useful for tracing dates of death and also burial places, especially in municipal cemeteries in which case the plot and grave number will usually also be given.

Although memorial cards are usually found among family papers, some have found their way into the hands of collectors who allow searches to be carried out in their databases, such as www.roscommonhistory.ie/Misc/Memorials/Misc.htm. Others find their way onto the second-hand market, often for sale via online auction sites.

You may also discover undertaker's bills in your family collection and these shed light on funeral arrangements. Those for my great-grandmother Emily Harriet Heritage, who died in 1924, show that her body was removed from the Central Home, Leytonstone, where she died, and give full details of her coffin and funeral procession, which comprised a horse-drawn hearse and a horse-drawn mourning coach behind it. I also found papers relating to the opening of the Heritage burial plot in Woodgrange Park Cemetery, East Ham, and these gave details of when the grave was reopened for later burials, including who was buried on those occasions and even the date of probate for my grandfather's will.

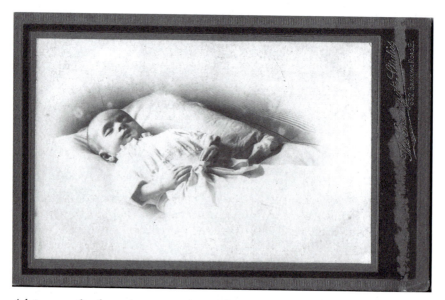

A late example of a post-mortem photo. This is of my uncle Clarence Heritage, who died in 1916. (Author's collection)

Post-mortem photo circa 1862. (Photo courtesy of Pat Brady)

Occasionally you may even discover a 'post-mortem photograph'. These were photographs of a loved one taken after death. They are most often to be found dating from the mid- to late nineteenth century and usually consist of a peaceful shot of the deceased in repose with his eyes shut. Sometimes they take the form of a studio shot of several family members, with the deceased posed in as lifelike a position as possible. Although the idea of post-mortem photographs seems rather creepy to us today, they were intended as keepsakes, often where no image of the deceased had been created during his lifetime. From the 1860s new developments in photography meant it was easier to produce multiple prints of a photo-graph and post-mortem photos were sometimes posted to family members.

Tontines

A tontine was an investment scheme whereby a group of subscribers contributed an initial sum of money (often a loan to the government) and then shared the interest from it between them. As members died the amount of interest the survivors received grew, until the sole survivor received all of it. Alternatively the tontine ran until a specific date when the remaining subscribers shared the proceeds between them. The government organized eleven schemes along these lines as a way of raising money in the seventeenth and eighteenth centuries, while other tontines were sometimes organized by local corporate boroughs. Subscribers usually invested on behalf of a young family member, because the longer a person lived the greater the profits. Tontine records usually give dates of death of subscribers and nominees as well as other details such as addresses, extracts from wills and ages. TNA has records relating to eighteenth-century government tontines under NDO 2 and NDO 3 with some in E 401, 403, 406-7. Both the British Library and SOG have indexes of subscribers to many of the government schemes. Francis L. Leeson's book *Guide to the Records of British State Tontines and Life Annuities of the 17th and 18th Centuries* (1968) is the most authoritative source for finding out more about these records.

Hatchments

If your ancestors were armigerous (had the right to bear a coat of arms) a hatchment may survive. This was a display of the deceased's arms and heraldic insignia, usually constructed from wood and canvas. In most cases canvas would be stretched over a diamond shaped wooden base and the heraldic display painted onto it. Hatchments were originally hung outside the family home for up to a year after the death, but many were later transferred to the parish church where today they may be seen hanging proudly on the wall or be hidden away in a dusty corner.

If you have knowledge of heraldry (see Chapter 3 for suggested intro-ductory books on the subject) the coat of arms on the hatchment will often enable you to trace the person's pedigree. Even without this knowledge, it is easy to determine the deceased's marital status at death from the back-ground colour of the hatchment as follows:

Spinster, Widow, Widower: black background
Married man: right half of background is white
Married woman: left half of background white

Hatchment in Lamberhurst Church, Kent, made on the death of Lydia Catherine Marriott, wife of William Alexander Morland of Court Lodge, Lamberhurst, in 1843. (Author's collection)

There is an excellent series of books entitled *Hatchments in Britain* edited by Peter Summers and John Titterton (Phillimore, 1974–2001) that provides an almost comprehensive survey of surviving hatchments at the time the series was written, although some hatchments have sadly disappeared since this time. The series has now been digitized and updated, and in this form is available on CD in major research libraries.

The hatchment shown above hangs in Lamberhurst Church, Kent, and using *Hatchments in Britain* I was able to determine that it was made on the death of Lydia Catherine Marriott, wife of William Alexander Morland of Court Lodge, Lamberhurst in 1843. She was the daughter of Revd James Marriott, Rector of Horsmonden. The coat of arms on the main shield of the hatchment portrays the arms of Morland. Those on the smaller shield depict Lydia's side of the family: the Marriotts, Pearsons and Bosworths. The fact that her arms are placed on a smaller escutcheon in the centre of the shield shows that she has no surviving brothers and is her father's heir.

The motto 'Resurgam' is frequently found on hatchments and means 'I will rise again'. Two cherubs' heads can be seen above the coat of arms and these were a regular feature of hatchments.

157

Court Rolls

Court rolls form part of the group of records we call 'manorial records' and are one of the least used sources by genealogists. This is a great shame as they have much information to offer.

The rolls recorded the proceedings of the manorial 'court baron' and as such covered a great variety of affairs relating to the administration of the manor. One of the most important types of entry for genealogists are the transfers of 'customary' or 'copyhold' land. This was a form of land tenure whereby the tenant held land from the lord of the manor, originally in return for agricultural work on the lord's land, but from the sixteenth century onwards in return for monetary payments. When a tenant died the court rolls would note that he had died since the last sitting of the court and his heir would usually be admitted to the tenancy. The entries provide important genealogical information, such as who was the son of whom and sometimes details of other family relationships. Occasionally you may also find an extract from the deceased tenant's will and this is very useful if the will itself has not survived in the records of the probate courts. Successive runs of court rolls can provide a lengthy pedigree. Although your ancestor's death might be recorded in one court roll, you may find further details of the admission of his heir in a later roll, so check all rolls you can find. The records can provide vital information; clarifying relationships where early baptismal entries give insufficient detail, or where the surname you are researching is heavily localized and there is more than one person with the same name.

Here is an example taken from the printed transcript of the *Courts of the Manors of Bandon and Beddington 1498–1552* by Hedley Marne Gowns, M. Wilks and J. Bray (London Borough of Sutton Libraries and Arts Services, 1983).

> John Dawborn, who held freely of the lord a tenement with garden adjacent for fealty and a rent of 20d, . . . has died . . . since the last court. . . . Joan, late wife of the said John and now wife of William Wylkynson has the aforementioned tenement with garden for the term of her life. And moreover . . . . Robert Dawborn is her eldest son and heir and is nine years old.

Up to the early 1700s the rolls will be in heavily abbreviated Latin and are hard to read, but from 1733 they will be in English and are relatively easy to decipher. The main problems with these records are that survival rates are patchy and locating them is not always straightforward. Many are deposited in record offices but some remain in the archives of landed families. All that are known to survive are listed in the Manorial Documents Register (MDR) at TNA. Part of the MDR is available at

158

www.nationalarchives.gov.uk/mdr which also provides some excellent background reading on manorial records. Where the county you seek is not yet online a trip to TNA is recommended. You can also use the A2A catalogue to search, which covers record office listings from across the country. It is important not to rely solely on local record office listings as many manorial documents are located in archives many miles away from where the manor was situated. This is because the lord of the manor may have held estates in several counties. John West has a very helpful list of court rolls, and other manorial records, that have been published in *Town Records* (3rd edn, Phillimore, 1997).

Further information on court rolls and other manorial records can be found at www.lancs.ac.uk/fass/projects/manorialrecords or in Mary Ellis' book *Using Manorial Records* (Public Record Office Readers Guide, 1997).

Inquisition post mortem (IPM)

Another manorial record was the 'inquisition post mortem' or 'escheat'. This was an inquiry undertaken on behalf of the crown after the death of a 'tenant in chief', someone who held land directly from the king (usually a lord of the manor). The inquiry established which lands he held and who his heir was. They survive from around 1240 until 1660 and their object was to discover how much income the lord's estate brought in, in order to calculate what was due to the crown in the form of tax or services. They will give the date of death of the lord and although, generally speaking, this source is of little use unless your ancestor was a lord of the manor, they may mention other people who lived on the manor in passing.

Many have been published and there is currently an Inquistion Post Mortem Project run by Winchester university (www.winchester.ac.uk) which aims to make all the surviving IPMs from 1236 to 1447 and from 1485 to 1509 freely available online in fully searchable texts.

Chapter 8

REPERCUSSIONS OF DEATH AND READING BETWEEN THE LINES

Finding a death is the full stop in our ancestor's life and we have seen just how much important information can be learned from death records. It also pays to pause and consider each ancestor's death in turn and whether or not there were any repercussions as a result of it. These may have been long-term or relatively short-lived: pausing to think about them can add flesh to the bare bones of our family tree while, if it does nothing else, it will provide food for thought. The purpose of this chapter is to give you some points to mull over.

Premature Death of a Parent

The premature death of one or both parents while there were still dependent children inevitably had massive repercussions for the family concerned. In the case of Edwin Barnes we saw how the remaining family was torn apart: Mary Ann's life in particular was greatly affected by Edwin's early demise. For each of your ancestors (both male and female) you should routinely consider the following:

- How old was he or she at death?
- Were they the sole, or main, breadwinner?
- Were there any surviving dependants?

If there were dependent children, try to find out what happened to them, and the other spouse, afterwards. With a little thought and research you can usually build up a picture of how deeply the family was affected by a premature death. From 1841 it is usually easy to trace the remaining family members via the census and this will give an indication of their circumstances. You can make a judgement as to how well they were coping based on factors such as whether or not they were sharing their house with another family, by the occupation of the remaining parent, and by noting whether any young children were sent out to work. In my experience, a greater number of widows than widowers seem to have chosen to 'go it alone' rather than remarry if they still had young children to care for, but they would almost always be forced to work hard to survive, whether they had a poorly paid cleaning job or whether they were middle-class women who took over the reins of a late husband's business.

Several women in my family have been left to bring up a family as a single parent because of the premature death of their spouse. How easily they coped largely depended on how well off they were. Sarah Barnes was poor and her daughter ended up in an orphanage, while the two elder children were sent out to work. All trace of Sarah disappears and it is frustrating not to know what happened to her in the end. By contrast, when my great-great-grandmother Elizabeth Heritage was widowed aged thirty-nine in 1857, although she had five children under the age of thirteen, she was in a much better position than Sarah because she came from a fairly well-off middle-class family. It is likely that her own father may have given her some financial support (although I have as yet found no evidence of this), but there is no doubt that she received help from her father-in-law, who left legacies to her and the children in his will nine years later. Even so life cannot have been easy. Her husband William had run a grocer's shop in Studley, near Redditch, and had recently taken over the post office when he died. I looked at local tax records both before and after William's death: they indicated that Elizabeth remained in the same house. The 1861 census describes her as running a 'Post Office, grocer and draper's shop' and so Elizabeth replaced William, not just as head of the family, but as head of the business too.

I was surprised to find, however, that by 1871 Elizabeth had left Studley and was in Birmingham running a grocer's shop with her son Thomas, aged nineteen, as her assistant. Investigation of the 1871 Studley census showed that Henry Johnson, who had no apparent connections to my family, took over the post office and grocer's shop in Studley after Elizabeth. Was this move made because she felt unable to continue in business in Studley, or was it an opportunity to move on to bigger, better things and possibly to start her son off in his own business in a more prosperous area? I will probably never know, but I can safely say that, without the premature death of her husband, Elizabeth would never have been in a position where she was running her own business. By 1881 Elizabeth had returned to Studley and was living with a cousin. She is described as a 'retired shopkeeper' and to me this, and the move to Birmingham, indicates that after William's death she had enjoyed the challenge of running her own business, and made it her calling.

Elizabeth's widowhood seems to have been a success story in many ways but, by contrast, your ancestor and her family may have ended up in the workhouse, or have received poor relief from the parish in order to survive. Try tracking them down using workhouse records or, before 1834, records of the Overseers of the Poor (kirk sessions records in Scotland). Records relating to the poor are abundant and often very informative. If your bereaved family disappears, remember to search for them on passenger lists. They may well have emigrated, especially if there were other family members already abroad who could give them a helping hand.

How did an early death of a parent affect the children?

Apart from the obvious consequences of the family being short of food and money, also consider the possible psychological effect the loss of a parent could have. We have seen how Mary Ann Barnes was described as a 'sad person' by those who knew her, but even the bereaved middle-class family must have been affected by their father or mother's early demise. Elizabeth Heritage's youngest son was only eighteen months old when his father died. As an adult he served a spell in Pentonville jail for stealing postal orders during his employment with the post office. His own death was as a result of an alcohol-related disease and I can but wonder if the lack of a father's firm hand in his upbringing, potentially combined with too little attention from his busy mother, were partly to blame.

Permanent Dependants

I have stressed how important it is to research the wider family rather than just your direct ancestors. In the course of this you may discover relatives who were disabled. The records in which you will usually spot a reference to their disability are the census returns. Depending on their handicap, they may have been permanently dependent on other family members.

In this case stop and consider what would have happened to the disabled person after the death of their parents. Did a sibling step in and take care of them or were they relegated to an institution? How did the care they required affect the rest of the family? Following up on such clues can often shed further light on your family history. On my own tree I noticed a young girl on the 1871 census who was shown as deaf and dumb. Born in 1855, her name was Vashti Clapson, the ninth and youngest child of John Clapson, a farm labourer, and his wife Harriet. They lived in Cranbrook, Kent, and looked after Vashti until their deaths in 1879 and 1880 respectively. I wondered what became of her after this.

The census showed that in 1881 and 1891 she was living with her sister Emma Carey and husband William in London. By 1890, however, Emma and William had started their own family, with one girl born that year, and another in 1892. Maybe this was the reason that by 1901 Vashti was in the workhouse in Tonbridge. Was it just too much trouble to continue looking after her when Emma had children to care for? Perhaps she and William could no longer afford to pay for Vashti's upkeep, or perhaps Vashti had behavioural problems caused by her deafness which led to placement in the workhouse. She died in the workhouse three years later with her death being registered by another sister.

Causes of Death

We looked at causes of death in Chapter 1, but it often pays to think more deeply about the cause of an ancestor's death. Some diseases were connected to certain occupations and in many cases this was not recognized by medical professionals until the twentieth century. Take a look at your ancestor's cause of death in conjunction with the job he did to see if there could be a connection. Lung diseases were caused by a multitude of occupations, but those particularly susceptible included mill workers, miners and also glass engravers, who inhaled silica particles. In many cases the cause of death would simply be given as 'bronchitis' and the clue that this was a result of lung disease, rather than an acute attack of bronchitis, will be where the certificate indicates the illness had lasted eight weeks or more. In this case, if your ancestor worked in one of these industries and died at a relatively young age, there is a fair chance his death was connected to his job. Similarly, dye workers were susceptible to bladder cancer, and skin diseases prevailed in those who came into direct contact with chemicals. Hatters might suffer from mercury poisoning because mercury was used to stiffen the felt used to make hats. This caused symptoms such as sore gums, numbness in the feet and hands, kidney damage, hallucinations and also depression with suicidal tendencies: hence the saying 'mad as a hatter'! Occasionally you may see a certificate that actually gives the cause of death as 'hatter's disease', but in many cases the symptoms of the disease, rather than the cause, were listed, while it might also be recorded as 'Bright's disease', a term that covered various forms of kidney damage.

Suicide was a cause of great shame for a family until relatively recent times. We have seen how inquest juries frequently endeavoured not to bring a verdict of suicide for this very reason. By looking at the cause of death on a certificate in tandem with any surviving inquest records you can, however, often read between the lines to ascertain whether or not a person did actually take his own life. As a girl I was lucky enough to meet a niece of my great-grandmother. She was very old, but managed to pass on much useful family history information. Foremost among it was her belief that her great-uncle had committed suicide. She was only six at the time but told me that no one would ever speak about his death. His death certificate stated that he died through drowning in the local river, but the inquest report showed that the river was actually only a few inches deep at the place where he drowned! It also indicated that he had financial worries and, putting all the evidence together, it is extremely likely that my informant was absolutely correct in her assumption.

Genetics

Another point to consider is genetics. One of the first questions you will be asked when you join a new doctor's practice is whether there is any history of certain diseases in your family. We usually take this as referring to our parents or possibly our grandparents, but this can be taken even further. It is fascinating to see if there is any link between the causes of death of earlier relatives and diseases that still affect the family today. We have seen that Thomas Heritage took his own life in 1904 and one of the reasons given was that he suffered from extremely painful chronic eczema. Interestingly one of his modern-day descendants also suffered from extremely bad eczema as a child. We can also apply this to diseases that do not actually kill. During the writing of this book I was in contact with someone who told me how scoliosis (a lateral curvature of the spine) runs in the Wintersgill branch of her family. During the course of her research she has made contact with other family members and it seems that the common ancestor who carried the gene for this condition must have been born in about 1700. It is highly likely, of course, that the original carrier lived at a much earlier date, but the family tree has not yet been traced past this point.

Job Vacancies

Finally, if the deceased was a craftsman or tradesman of any sort, try to find out who took his place in the community after his death. Although some widows carried on their late husbands' businesses, many were not able or prepared to do so. In many cases a new tradesman would have stepped in to fill his shoes, especially in a small village where he was the only person plying that particular trade or craft. It's worth trying to find out who this was; it may have been another family member. When my ancestor Edward Dickinson, a miller in the small hamlet of Garnett Bridge, died prematurely in 1821, his cousin James moved into the village to take over the mill. I initially noticed that James started baptizing his children in the local church and presumed that he was helping Edward's widow Mary run the mill. However, in 1834 the mill was put up for sale and the auction notice in the local paper makes it clear that James was the tenant and as such would have been paying Mary rent. Therefore, although I knew that by 1851 Mary was running a guest house in Kendal, this indicated that she had probably moved her family away from Garnett Bridge much sooner than I thought and possibly soon after Edward's death. Investigating what happened to the mill after Edward's death gave me a clearer indication of what happened to his family.

Likewise, if your family suddenly moves to a new parish, it could well have been to fill such a gap. This seems to be the case when the Dickinsons first moved to Garnett Bridge in the early 1800s. The burial records reveal the death of one of the millers there a short time before and it is likely that my family bought his business.

So death had certain knock-on effects. It may have thrown a family onto the poverty line or caused them to move away, or even emigrate. On the other hand some deaths were beneficial. The death of an elderly dependent parent may have meant fewer mouths to feed and may have given the family more space or the freedom to move away if desired. On the other hand, they may have lost a vital carer for the younger children, whose presence had allowed the mother to undertake employment outside the home. By thinking along these lines, although we often provoke further unanswered questions on the way, we can begin to see a much broader picture of the lives our ancestors lived.

NOTES

Chapter 1
1. See www.histpop.org for the full text of both Registration Acts and the Registrar General's Annual Reports.
2. Statistics from the Division of Reproductive Health, National Centre for Chronic Disease Prevention and Health Promotion, Centres for Disease Control and Prevention journal. Issue 48(38) pages 849-858. Published 1 October 1999. Although these statistics relate to the USA they are mirrored in the UK.

Chapter 2
1. From the collections of Kent History and Library Centre. Yalding Burial Register CKS-P45/1/1
2. Quotation courtesy of Ancestry.com .
3. Quotation included by kind permission of Suffolk Record Office, Bury St Edmunds (SROB FL612/4/8).
4. From the collections of Kent History and Library Centre CKS-P20/1/8.
5. Hugh Mellor and Brian Parsons, *London Cemeteries. An Illustrated Guide* (4th edition, The History Press, 2008)

Chapter 4
1. Shakespeare Birthplace Trust Library and Archive ER 10/5/177.

Chapter 6
1. Karen Grannum and Nigel Taylor, *Wills and Probate Records. A guide for family historians,* (TNA, 2nd edn, 2009).
2. WRW/K will of Agnes Williamson 1811. Transcript by permission of the Archives Service Manager, Lancashire Archives.
3. The wills of Thomas and Margaret Sacre are from the collections at Kent History and Library Centre references PRC 17/21/99 and PRC 17/26/334 respectively.
4. The National Archives (TNA) IR 26/313.
5. Lancashire Record Office, Preston ref: WRW/K George Stewardson 1807.

Appendix

USEFUL ADDRESSES

British Library
96 Euston Road, London
NW1 2DB
www.bl.uk

British Library Newspapers
Colindale Avenue
London
NW9 5HE
www.bl.uk/welcome/newspapers.html

Commonwealth War Graves Commission
2 Marlow Road
Maidenhead
SL6 7DX
www.cwgc.org

Federation of Family History Societies
PO BOX 8857
Lutterworth
LE17 9BJ
www.ffhs.org.uk

General Register Office
PO BOX 2
Southport
PR8 2JD
To order certificates:
www.gro.gov.uk/gro/content/certificates/default.asp

Institute of Heraldic and Genealogical Studies
79-81 Northgate
Canterbury
CT1 1BA
www.ihgs.ac.uk

London Family History Centre
64-68 Exhibition Road
London
SW7 2PA
www.londonfhc.org

London Metropolitan Archives
40 Northampton Road
London
EC1R 0HB
www.cityoflondon.gov.uk/lma

The National Archives
Ruskin Avenue
Kew, Richmond
TW9 4DE
www.nationalarchives.gov.uk

National Library of Wales
Aberystwyth
SY23 3BU
www.llgc.org.uk

Society of Genealogists
14 Charterhouse Buildings
Goswell Road
London
EC1M 7 BA
www.sog.org.uk

Scotland
National Records of Scotland
HM General Register House
2 Princes Street
Edinburgh
EH1 3YY
www.nrscotland.gov.uk
For information about the GRO for Scotland and National Archives of
Scotland websites see the note under the Quick Reference and Useful
Websites section.

Scotlandspeople Centre
HM General Register House
2 Princes Street
Edinburgh
EH1 3YY
www.scotlandspeoplehub.gov.uk

National Library of Scotland
57 George IV Bridge
Edinburgh
EH1 1EW
www.nls.uk

Ireland
National Archives of Ireland
Bishops Street,
Dublin 8
www.nationalarchives.ie

National Library of Ireland
Kildare Street
Dublin 2
www.nli.ie

General Register Office of Ireland Government Offices
Convent Road
Roscommon
www.groireland.ie

General Register Office of Ireland – Public Reading Room
3rd Floor, Block 7
Irish Life Centre
Lower Abbey Street
Dublin 1

Public Record Office Northern Ireland
2 Titanic Boulevard
Belfast
BT3 9HQ
www.proni.gov.uk

General Register Office for Northern Ireland
Oxford House
49-55 Chichester Street
Belfast
BT1 4HL
www.nidirect.gov.uk/gro

BIBLIOGRAPHY

General

Adolph, Anthony, *Tracing Your Family History* (Collins, 2004)

Bevan, Amanda, *Tracing Your Ancestors in the National Archives* (7th edition, 2006)

Hey, David *Journeys In Family History* (2nd edition, 2004)

Herber, Mark, *Ancestral Trails* (Sutton Publishing, 2004)

Humphery-Smith, Cecil, (ed) *The Phillimore's Atlas and Index of Parish Registers* (Phillimore, 2003)

Maxwell, Ian, *How To Trace Your Irish Ancestors* (2nd edition, How To Books Ltd, 2009)

Paley, Ruth and Fowler, Simon, *Family Skeletons* (The National Archives, 2005)

Paton, Chris, *Researching Scottish Family History* (The Family History Partnership, 2010)

Raymond, Stuart, A., *Death and Burial Records for Family Historians* (The Family History Partnership, 2011)

Rogers, Colin, *The Family Tree Detective* (3rd edition, Manchester University Press, 1997)

Death Certificates

Foster, Mike W., *'A Comedy of Errors' or The Marriage Records of England and Wales 1837-1899* (M. Foster, 1998)

Foster, Mike W., *'A Comedy of Errors Act 2' or The Marriage Records of England and Wales 1837-1899* (M. Foster, 2002)

Gibson, Jeremy, *Electoral Registers 1832-1948 and Burgess Rolls* (The Family History Partnership, 2008)

Grundy, J. E., *A Dictionary of Medical and Related Terms for the Family Historian* (Swansong Publications, 2006)

Hey, David, *The Oxford Guide to Family History* (Oxford University Press, 2002)

Jolly, Emma, *Tracing Your British Indian Ancestors* (Pen and Sword, 2012)

Langston, Brett, *A Handbook to the Civil Registration Districts of England and Wales* (Family History Partnership, 2nd edition, 2003).

Wiggins, Ray, *Registration Districts* (Society of Genealogists, 3rd edition, 2001)

Yeo, Tim, *The British Overseas: a guide to records of their births, baptisms, marriages, deaths and burials available in the United Kingdom* (3rd edition, Guildhall Library, 1994)

Causes of Death and Old Medical Terms (Spindrift Printing and Publishing, 2002). Available from www.genealogyprinters.com.

Burials

Breed, Geoffrey R., *My Ancestors Were Baptists* (4th edition Society of Genealogists 2002)

Brooke Little, James, *The Law of Burial: including all the Burial Acts* (3rd edition, Shaw and Sons, London, 1902)

Gibbens, Lilian, *Using Death and Burial Records for Family Historians* (Federation of Family History Societies, 1997)

Joseph, Dr Antony, *My Ancestors Were Jewish* (4th edition, Family History Partnership, 2008)

Leary, William, *My Ancestors Were Methodists* (Society of Genealogists, 1999)

McLaughlin, Eve, *Nonconformist Ancestors* (Varney's Press, 1995)

Meller, H., and Parsons, B., *London Cemeteries* (4th edition, The History Press, 2008)

Milligan, Edward H., and Thomas, Malcom J., *My Ancestors Were Quakers* (Society of Genealogists, 1999)

Ruston, Alan, *My Ancestors Were English Presbyterians/Unitarians* (Society of Genealogists, 1993)

Steel, D.J., *The National Index of Parish Registers Vol 3* (Phillimore, *1974)*

Steel, D.J., *The National Index of Parish Registers Vol 5* (Phillimore, *1976)*

Gravestones and Monumental Inscriptions

Bailey, Brian, *Churchyards of England and Wales* (Robert Hale Ltd, 1987)

Burgess, Frederick, *English Churchyard Memorials* (Lutterworth Press, 1963)

Fearn, Jacqueline, *Discovering Heraldry* (Discovering Books, 2006)

Taylor, Richard, *How to Read A Church* (Rider, 2003)

Vincent, W.T., *In Search of Gravestones Old and Curious* (Mitchell and Hughes, London, 1896) Also online at www.gutenberg.org/ebooks/12978

Webb, Clifford, and Wolfston, Pat, *Greater London Cemeteries and Crematoria* (3rd edition, Society of Genealogists, 1994)

Wilsher, Betty, *Understanding Scottish Gravestones* (W.R. Chambers Ltd, 2nd edition, 1995)

Inquest Records

Gibson, Jeremy, and Rogers, Colin, *Coroners' Records in England and Wales* (3rd edition, The Family History Partnership, 2009)

Gibson, Jeremy, *Quarter Sessions Records for Family Historians* (5th edition, The Family History Partnership, 2007)

Greenwald, Maria W., and Gary I., *Coroners' Inquests: a source of vital statistics: Westminster 1761-1866* (The Journal of Legal Medicine, Vol 4, number 1, 1983, p 51-86)

Hawkings, David T., *Criminal Ancestors* (The History Press, 2009)

Hunnisett, R. F., *The Medieval Coroner* (Cambridge University Press, 1961)

Hunnisett, R. F., *Sussex Coroners' Inquests 1458-1558* (Sussex Record Society, 1985).

Hunnisett, R. F., *Sussex Coroners' Inquests 1458-1558* (Sussex Record Society, Vol LXXIV, 1985)

Hunnisett, R. F., *Sussex Coroners' Inquests 1558-1603* (Public Record Office, 1996)

Hunnisett, R. F., *Sussex Coroners' Inquests 1603-1688* (Public Record Office, 1998)

Hunnisett, R. F., *Wiltshire Coroners' Bills 1752–1796* (Wiltshire Record Society, Vol 36)

Purchase, W.B., *Sir John Jervis on the Office and Duties of Coroners* (8th edition, Sweet and Maxwell, London)

Thurston, Gavin, *Coroner's Practice* (Butterworth and Co. Ltd, London, 1958)

Newspapers

Griffiths, Dennis, *The Encyclopedia of the British Press 1422-1992* (Macmillan Press, 1992)

West, John, *Town Records* (Phillimore, 1983)

Gibson, Jeremy, Langston, Brett and Smith, Brenda W., *Local Newspapers 1750-1920* (2nd edition, Federation of Family History Societies, 2002)

Logan, Roger, *Friendly Society Records* (Federation of Family History Societies, 2000)

Murphy, Michael, *Newspapers and Local History* (Phillimore, 1991)

Westmancoat, John, *Newspapers* (The British Library Board, 1985)

Wills

Arkell, T., Evans, N., Goose, N., (eds) *When Death Us Do Part* (Leopard's Head Press Ltd, 2000)

Grannum, Karen, and Taylor, Nigel, *Wills and Probate Records. A guide for family historians* (2nd edition, The National Archives, 2009)

Gibson, Jeremy and Churchill, Else, *Probate Jurisdictions: Where to Look for Wills* (5th edition, Federation of Family History Societies, 2002)

Raymond, Stuart A., *Words from Wills and other probate records* (Federation of Family History Societies, 2004)

Scott, Miriam, *Index to Dorset wills and administrations proved in the PCC, 1812–1858* (Somerset and Dorset Family History Society, 1992)

West, John, *Village Records* (Phillimore, 1997)

Wright, David, Kent *Probate Records. A Catalogue and Practical Guide* (D. Wright, 2004)

Miscellany

Leeson, Francis L., Guide *to the Records of British State Tontines and Life Annuities of the 17th and 18th Centuries* (Pinhorns, 1968)

Summers, Peter, and Titterton, John, *Hatchments in Britain Vol 5* (Phillimore, 1985)

Ellis, Mary, *Using Manorial Records* (Public Record Office Readers Guide, 1997)

Park, Peter B., *My Ancestors Were Manorial Tenants* (Society of Genealogists, 1990)

Gowans, H.M., Wilks, M., and Bray, J., *The Courts of the Manors of Bandon and Beddington 1498-1552* (London Borough of Sutton Libraries and Arts Services, 1983).

INDEX